FRIENDS
OF ACPL

7/10

PA̲̅ECTION

Learn Every Day About Animals

Edited by Kathy Charner

D0870714

Learn Every Day About ANIMALS

100 BEST IDEAS from TEACHERS

EDITED BY
Kathy Charner

© 2010 Gryphon House, Inc.
Published by Gryphon House, Inc.
10770 Columbia Pike, Suite 201
Silver Spring, MD 20901
800.638.0928; 301.595.9500; 301.595.0051 (fax)

Visit us on the web at www.gryphonhouse.com

All rights reserved. No part of this publication may be reproduced, stored in a retrieval system, or transmitted in any form or by any means, electronic, mechanical, photocopying, recording or otherwise, without the prior written permission of the publisher. Printed in the United States of America. Every effort has been made to locate copyright and permission information.

Illustrations: Deb Johnson

Library of Congress Cataloging-in-Publication Information:
Learn every day about animals / edited by Kathy Charner.
    p. cm.
 ISBN 978-0-87659-126-0
 1. Animals—Juvenile literature. I. Charner, Kathy.
 QL49.l3725 2010
 590—dc22
                                    2009051770

BULK PURCHASE

Gryphon House books are available for special premiums and sales promotions as well as for fund-raising use. Special editions or book excerpts also can be created to specification. For details, contact the Director of Marketing at Gryphon House.

DISCLAIMER

Gryphon House, Inc. and the author cannot be held responsible for damage, mishap, or injury incurred during the use of or because of activities in this book. Appropriate and reasonable caution and adult supervision of children involved in activities and corresponding to the age and capability of each child involved is recommended at all times. Do not leave children unattended at any time. Observe safety and caution at all times.

Table of Contents

Note: The books listed in the Related Children's Books section of each activity may occasionally include books that are only available used or through your local library.

Introduction

You have in your hands a great teacher resource! This book, which is part of the *Learn Every Day* series, contains 100 activities you can use with children ages 3–6 to help them develop a lifelong love of learning, as well as the knowledge and skills all children need to become successful students in kindergarten and beyond. The activities in this book are written by teachers and professionals from the field of early childhood education—educators and professionals who use these activities in their classrooms every day.

The activities in the books are separated by curriculum areas, such as Art, Dramatic Play, Outdoor Play, Transitions, and so on, and are organized according to their age appropriateness, so activities appropriate for children age three and up come first, then activities appropriate for children age four and up, and finally, activities for children age five and up. Each activity has the following components—learning objectives, a list of related vocabulary words, a list of thematically related books, a list of the materials (if any) you need to complete the activity, directions for preparation and the activity itself. Also included in each activity is an assessment component to help you observe how well the children are meeting the learning objectives. Given the emphasis on accountability in early childhood education, these assessment strategies are essential.

Several activities also contain teacher-to-teacher tips that provide smart and useful ideas, including how to expand the central idea of an activity in a new way or where to find the materials necessary to complete a given activity. Some activities also include related fingerplays, poems, or songs that you can sing and chant with the children. Children love singing, dancing, and chanting. These actions help expand a child's understanding of an activity's learning objectives.

This book and the other books in this series give early childhood educators 100 great activities that require few materials and little if any preparation. These activities are sure to make learning fun and engaging for children.

Colorful Cows

LEARNING OBJECTIVES

The children will:

1. Identify a cow.
2. Identify colors.
3. Use markers and crayons to color cows.
4. Express creativity through coloring.

Materials

cow shapes cut out
   from white
   construction
   paper
markers and
   crayons

VOCABULARY

black	brown	crayon	marker	purple	yellow
blue	cow	green	orange	red	

PREPARATION

● Place the paper cow shapes, markers, and crayons in the art center.

WHAT TO DO

1. Ask the children to identify the shape of their papers. Ask if any of the children have seen a real cow before. What color was it?
2. Ask the children to identify the colors of the crayons and markers.
3. Suggest that the children draw faces and other features on their cows. They can draw spots and patches if they like.
4. Have the children color their cows. Encourage the children to use a variety of colors.

TEACHER-TO-TEACHER TIP

● Cover a bulletin board in your classroom with green cloth or butcher paper. Add a red paper barn to create a farm scene. Once the children's colorful cows are complete, arrange them in the "pasture" for the children and families to enjoy.

POEM

Colorful Cows by Laura Wynkoop

I've never seen a yellow cow,   *I think it would be neat to see*
Or one that's green or blue.   *A purple cow say, "Moo."*

ASSESSMENT

Consider the following:

● Can the children name the colors they used in their pictures?
● Can the children identify the shape of their paper? Can they find other cows in the room?

Laura Wynkoop, San Dimas, CA

Children's Books

Bessie the Black and White Cow by Bob Gross
Big Red Barn by Margaret Wise Brown
Open the Barn Door by Christopher Santoro
There's a Cow in the Cabbage Patch by Clare Beaton

Making a Cow Bell

3+

LEARNING OBJECTIVES

The children will:
1. Create a cow bell.
2. Develop their small motor skills.
3. Learn about the function of cow bells.
4. Shake their cow bells to the rhythm of an action rhyme.

Materials

pictures of cows
small bells
ribbon
child-safe scissors
felt pens
stickers

VOCABULARY

colors	decorate	ribbon	wrist
cow	rhyme	sound	
cow bell	rhythm	stickers	

WHAT TO DO

1. Set out several pictures of cows and talk to the children about cows. Ask the children, "Where do cows live?"
2. Explain to the children that they will be making their own cow bells. Say, "After we make our own special cow bells, then we can ring our cow bells to the action rhyme."
3. Ask the children to choose a color of ribbon for their bell.
4. Encourage the children to decorate their cow bells and ribbons by coloring or drawing on them or adding stickers.
5. Help the children either tie the cow bells to their wrists or just tie the ribbon so they can hold their bells.

6. Teach the children the action rhyme "Hey, Diddle, Diddle" and model how to shake a cow bell to the beat of the rhyme.

ASSESSMENT

Consider the following:
● Do the children decorate their cow bells?
● Can the children shake their cow bells in time with the rhythm of the action rhyme?

Children's Books

Big Red Barn by Margaret Wise Brown
Open the Barn Door by Christopher Santoro
There's a Cow in the Cabbage Patch by Clare Beaton

Lily Erlic, Victoria, British Columbia, Canada

Clay Ladybugs

LEARNING OBJECTIVES

The children will:
1. Learn the different body parts of a ladybug.
2. Practice small motor skills and following directions.

Materials

images of ladybugs
red and black clay
small wiggle eyes

VOCABULARY

abdomen	bug	jointed legs	thorax
antennae	head	ladybug	wings
black	insect	red	

WHAT TO DO

1. Engage the children in a discussion about ladybugs. Display images of ladybugs and their body parts. Talk to the children about the various body parts ladybugs (and all insects) have, including the head, pronotum (behind the head), thorax (middle section where legs are attached), abdomen (body behind the thorax where most of the organs are), wings, antennae, and legs.

2. Demonstrate how to roll a circular red body and a smaller black head.
3. Add black clay dots to the red body, black clay antennae to the head and wiggle eyes to the face.
4. As the children construct their own clay ladybugs, discuss the different body parts of ladybugs.

ASSESSMENT

Consider the following:
- How many sections does the body of a ladybug have? What are they called?
- How many antennae do ladybugs have?
- How many legs do ladybugs have?

Kimberly Hutmacher, Illiopolis, IL

Children's Books

Are You a Ladybug? by Judy Allen
A Ladybug's Life by John Himmelman
Ten Little Ladybugs by Melanie Gerth

Elephants Are Big!

4+

LEARNING OBJECTIVES

The children will:
1. Learn about elephants in zoos and in the wild.
2. Improve motor skills.
3. Develop color concepts including the color gray and mixing colors.
4. Learn about the big size of elephants.

Materials

various colors of
 paint, including
 black, white,
 brown, red,
 green, and blue
paintbrushes
aprons
easels
construction or
 other painting
 paper, some with
 elephant pictures
 and some plain
 so the children
 can make their
 own

VOCABULARY

big	elephant	nature	wild
color	gray	trunk	zoo
ears	mud	tusk	

PREPARATION

● Set out enough of the above materials for each child.

WHAT TO DO

1. Ask the children if they have seen an elephant. Was it in a zoo?
2. Encourage the children to talk about how big elephants are. Show the children images of elephants to help the discussion. What color are they? Do they have tusks? Do the children know anyone who has been to Africa or Asia and seen elephants in the wild? Are all elephants gray? If an elephant rolls in the mud, is it a different color? Why would an elephant roll in the mud? Encourage all the children to participate.
3. Show the children the materials and encourage each of them to paint an elephant. They can mix colors, such as black and white, to make gray. They can also paint in grass and the sky and use their imaginations.

TEACHER-TO-TEACHER TIP

● Have any of the teachers at the school, or parents or caretakers, observed elephants in the wild in Africa or Asia? If so, ask them to talk to the children about the experience.

ASSESSMENT

Consider the following:
● Can the child tell you where elephants live?
● Can the child describe an elephant, using color and other descriptors?

Shirley Anne Ramaley, Sun City, AZ

Children's Books

Elephants by
Melissa Stewart
*Elephants: A Book
for Children* by
Steve Bloom and
David Henry Wilson
Just for Elephants by
Carol Buckley
*"Stand Back," Said
the Elephant, "I'm
Going to Sneeze!"* by
Patricia Thomas

Playdough Porcupines

LEARNING OBJECTIVES

The children will:

1. Be creative with different art mediums.
2. Identify a porcupine.
3. Learn that porcupines have sharp quills.

Materials

playdough
ingredients (see
the recipe to the
right)
toothpicks
wiggle eyes
glue

VOCABULARY

playdough   porcupine   quills   toothpick

RECIPE

No-Cook Playdough   bowl
1 cup cold water   1 cup salt
2 teaspoons vegetable oil   brown tempera paint
3 cups flour   2 tablespoons cornstarch

- In a bowl, mix water, salt, oil, and enough tempera paint to make brown.
- Gradually add flour and cornstarch until the mixture reaches the consistency of bread dough.

PREPARATION

- Have all ingredients and materials ready.
- Read a book about porcupines with the children.

WHAT TO DO

1. Have the children assist in making playdough.
2. Take turns pouring, stirring, and kneading the dough.
3. Give each child toothpicks and about half a cup of playdough.
4. Ask the children to place the playdough on the table and mold an egg-shaped mound.
5. Have the children push toothpicks into the playdough to make quills. Have the children glue on two wiggle eyes.

TEACHER-TO-TEACHER TIP

- Use blunt-tipped toothpicks.

ASSESSMENT

Consider the following:

- Can the children measure and help make playdough?
- Can the children identify a porcupine and its quills?

Children's Books

*A Porcupine Named
Fluffy* by Helen Lester
Porcupine by Meg Tilly
*Porcupining:
A Prickly Love Story* by
Lisa Wheeler
*Welcome to the
World of Porcupines* by
Diane Swanson

Sandra Ryan, Buffalo, NY

Slithering Snakes

LEARNING OBJECTIVES

The children will:
1. Develop their small motor skills.
2. Learn how a snake moves.

Materials

many shades of
    green paper
child-safe scissors
brown paper
old neckties
dowel rods (at least
    four)
fiberfill
child-safe craft glue
    or fusible
    webbing or
    needle and
    thread
wiggle eyes
red felt

VOCABULARY

environment   slither   snake   tongue

PREPARATION

- Cut many shades of green paper into leaf shapes. (More advanced children can help with this step.)
- Use brown paper to create a large tree on the wall.
- Add the leaf shapes to the tree.

WHAT TO DO

1. Ask the children's families to send an old necktie. The busier the print on the tie, the better.
2. Cut open one of the tie's ends and fill with fiberfill. Use the dowel rods to poke the fiberfill in firmly.
3. Sew or have the children glue the end of the tie closed.
4. The children can add wiggle eyes and red felt cut into snake tongue shapes using craft glue or use the self-adhesive kind.
5. The children can sit under the tree and play with their snakes. What fun! Talk about how snakes move without legs and how they can even climb trees. Emphasize that the movement the snake uses to move is called "slithering."
6. Ask the children if they can slither. Clear a large floor area or go out into the hall and have "slither races" in which the children race each other while slithering like a snake.

ASSESSMENT

Consider the following:
- Observe the children as they stuff their snake. Do they have difficulty manipulating the materials?
- Can the children demonstrate the slithering motions?

Virginia Jean Herrod, Columbia, SC

Children's Books

Album of Snakes and Other Reptiles by Tom McGowen
Hide and Snake by Keith Baker
Snakes Slither and Hiss by D.K. Publishing

Stripes

4+

LEARNING OBJECTIVES

The children will:
1. Learn about animals that have spots and stripes.
2. Explore a painting technique.

Materials

paper
acrylic paints in
    yellow ochre,
    and black
paintbrushes
rag
water
bowls

VOCABULARY

design	spots	stripes
leopard	spotted deer	tiger

PREPARATION

● Draw or download and print the outline of a tiger on a sheet of paper. Prepare one paper for every child. (Encourage those children who are able to create their own.)

WHAT TO DO

1. Talk about animals having spots and stripes and other patterns on their bodies.
2. Distribute the papers. Let the children paint the tiger with yellow ochre, leaving the belly area white. Wait until the paint dries.
3. Encourage the children to dip their index finger in the black acrylic paint and drag it along the body of the tiger to create stripes.
4. The same exercise can be repeated for spotted animals like leopards and spotted deer. The children can dip their fingers in paint and tap it on the paper to make spots.
5. At snack time, let the children eat a striped sandwich by squirting ketchup across the sandwich.
6. Challenge the children to look at one another and identify who is wearing clothes with stripes and spots on them.

ASSESSMENT

Consider the following:
● Show pictures of assorted animals to the children and ask them to pick out animals with spots.
● Are the children able to use their fingers to make stripes?

Shyamala Shanmugasundaram, Nerul, Navi Mumbai, India

Children's Books

The Last Leopard by Lauren St. John
Time for Bed, Little Tiger by Julie Sykes
Why Do Tigers Have Stripes? by Helen Edom

Stuffed Animal

4+

LEARNING OBJECTIVES

The children will:
1. Listen fully and follow directions.
2. Develop competence and confidence using their hands.
3. Create three-dimensional works of art.

Materials

brown grocery bags
child-safe scissors
paper clips
crayons
markers
hole punch
yarn
newspaper

VOCABULARY

animal	front	lace up	shapes
back	holes	newspaper	stuffed animal
cut	identical	paper clip	

PREPARATION

● Depending on the children's skill level, you may choose to partially precut the animal shapes.

WHAT TO DO

1. Help the children draw and cut out two identical animal shapes from a brown grocery bag.
2. Decorate the front and back with animal features.
3. Place the two animal shapes together with paper clips and use a hole punch to make holes about 2" apart around the edge of the animal.
4. Show the children how to use yarn to lace up their animal and leave an opening for stuffing.
5. After they lace the animals up, the children can remove the paper clips and stuff the animals with newspaper. Finish lacing up the stuffed animal and tie the yarn ends together.

TEACHER-TO-TEACHER TIP

● Use simple shapes, such as an oval, for the animal's body.

Children's Books

Olivia and the Missing Toy by Ian Falconer
Tatty Ratty by Helen Cooper
What Does My Teddy Bear Do All Night? by Bruno Hachler

ASSESSMENT

Consider the following:
● Can the children listen to and follow directions?
● Can the children use scissors to cut out animal shapes, and yarn to lace up animal shapes?
● Can the children complete a three-dimensional project?

MaryLouise Alu Curto, Mercerville, NJ

Underwater Art

Materials

scrap paper and 1
   piece of plain
   white paper for
   each child
crayons
blue and green
   watercolor paints
paintbrushes

LEARNING OBJECTIVES

The children will:

1. Learn to draw simple underwater animals.
2. Practice using a crayon-resist art technique.

VOCABULARY

brush	draw	underwater
crayon	resist	watercolor

WHAT TO DO

1. Give each child a piece of plain paper and suggest that they use crayons to draw simple underwater plants and animals on the paper.
2. Tell the children that they should leave the background of their paper white and not color the water around the plants and animals with crayon, because you'll be using paints for that later.
3. When the children have finished coloring their plants and animals, distribute blue and green watercolor paints.
4. Tell the children to paint over their entire sheet of paper using a combination of blue and green watercolor paint. The paint will adhere to the paper, but not to the crayon (the crayon resist).

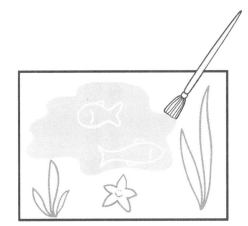

ASSESSMENT

Consider the following:

- Do the children draw and color underwater plants and animals?
- Do the children paint over the entire sheet of paper? Do the children enjoy painting over the paper?

Janet Hammond, Mount Laurel, NJ

Children's Books

At Home in the Coral Reef by Katy Muzik
How to Draw Underwater Animals by Rob Court
The Underwater Alphabet Book by Jerry Pallotta

Where Do Cows Live?

3+

LEARNING OBJECTIVES

The children will:
1. Learn where cows live.
2. Use blocks to build barns and cow pens.
3. Develop large and small motor skills.

Materials

photos or pictures
of barns and
farms
blocks in a variety
of shapes and
sizes
toy cows (optional)

VOCABULARY

cow	blocks	building	pen
barn	build	farm	

WHAT TO DO

1. Ask the children where they think cows live. Display photos or pictures of barns and farms and have the children describe the buildings they see.
2. Encourage the children to use blocks to make barns and cow pens.

TEACHER-TO-TEACHER TIP

- After the children have built their barns and cow pens, provide toy cows for them to play with in their block structures.

SONG

A Dairy Cow by Laura Wynkoop
(Tune: "Do You Know the Muffin Man?")
Oh, have you seen a dairy cow,
A dairy cow, a dairy cow?
Oh, have you seen a dairy cow
Inside a big red barn?

Oh, yes, I've seen a dairy cow,
A dairy cow, a dairy cow.
Oh, yes, I've seen a dairy cow
Inside a big red barn.

Children's Books

Big Red Barn by
Margaret Wise Brown
Open the Barn Door by
Christopher Santoro
*There's a Cow in
the Cabbage Patch* by
Clare Beaton

ASSESSMENT

Consider the following:
- Display photos of a farm, a jungle, and a city. Can the children identify where cows live?
- Can the children use the blocks to create barns and fences?

Laura Wynkoop, San Dimas, CA

Animal Pyramids

LEARNING OBJECTIVES

The children will:
1. Identify animals.
2. Build with blocks.
3. Think critically.
4. Practice problem solving.
5. Read sight words.

Materials

black permanent
  marker
pictures of animals
tape
large building
  block set

VOCABULARY

animal names	build	count	pyramid	tumble
blocks	building	crash	tower	

PREPARATION

- Use the black marker to write each animal name on each picture.
- Tape one animal picture to each building block.

WHAT TO DO

1. Demonstrate how to build a pyramid by displaying a set of five or more blocks in a row on the table.
2. Show how to stack a set of four blocks on top of that row, then three blocks, then two, then one.
3. Once the pyramid is built, read each animal name aloud, as you point to the animal words on the blocks.
4. Say "animal crash," remove one or more blocks from the bottom portion of the pyramid, and watch the blocks come tumbling down.
5. Set the materials at the blocks center and invite the children to work individually or with a partner as they repeat the activity.

ASSESSMENT

Consider the following:
- Cut block shapes from colored construction paper. Invite the children to glue the blocks to a sheet of art paper to form a pyramid. Allow the children to use rubber stamps to stamp an animal picture on each block. Write the animal name on each paper block. Invite the child to read the animal words aloud as you listen and assess their sight word recognition and animal recognition skills.
- Create a pyramid and have the child copy your pyramid. One by one, place blocks on the table. Watch the child as she imitates you. Observe to see how well the child can build a pyramid similar to yours. Take turns removing blocks from one another's pyramid from top to bottom as you read the animal names aloud.

Children's Books

1, 2, 3 to the Zoo: A Counting Book by Eric Carle
Brown Bear, Brown Bear, What Do You See? by Bill Martin, Jr.
The Farm Alphabet Book by Jane Miller
Understanding Farm Animals by Ruth Thomson

Mary J. Murray, Mazomanie, WI

BOOKS

Animals Are Growing

3+

The children will:
1. Learn to put animal pictures into sequence from smallest to largest.
2. Learn that all animals are born as babies and grow up.

Materials

pictures of various animals showing them from babies to fully grown (**Note:** It is best to use only three pictures for younger children to sequence; increase the number for older children.)
cardboard or poster board

VOCABULARY

| baby | bigger | growing | largest | size |
| big | discussion | large | sequence | small |

PREPARATION

- Find pictures of animals in coloring books, magazines, and catalogues. Place them on heavy cardboard or poster board and laminate them for durability.

WHAT TO DO

1. Place the pictures in the math area.
2. Read a book on the growth of an animal and then engage the children in a discussion about the growing process.
3. Encourage the children to use the pictures to sequence the animals' growth.

POEM

You're Growing by Eileen Lucas

When I was just a wee little baby
My parents said to me,
"My, how you're growing!"
Then when it was time to start school
My teacher said to me,
"My, how you're growing!"
I went out with my friends one day
And guess what they said to me?
"My, how you're growing!"
I was tired of people telling me
"My, how you're growing!"

So I went to visit my Nan and Pop
To see what they would say.
"Come here my child,
Have they been feeding you well?"
And before I had the chance to answer,
They gave me a bowl of cookies.
And then they said,
"Now eat all your cookies
So Mom and Dad can say,
'My, how you're growing!'"

Children's Books

The Baby Bunny by Margaret Hillert
Deep in the Swamp by Donna M. Bateman
The Furry Alphabet Book by Jerry Pallotta
The Mother's Day Mice by Eve Bunting

ASSESSMENT

Consider the following:
- Can the children see the growth of animals by sequencing the pictures from babies to fully grown?
- Can the children identify by name the animals in the images?

Eileen Lucas, Fort McMurray, Alberta, Canada

Barnyard Buddies

3+

LEARNING OBJECTIVES

The children will:
1. Learn about animals found on a farm.
2. Develop their listening skills.

Materials

On the Farm by Roger Priddy
cutouts of animals that appear in *On the Farm*

VOCABULARY

barn	duck	goose	pig
chicken	farm	horse	sheep
cow	farmer	lamb	

WHAT TO DO

1. Engage the children in a conversation about farms. Ask the children to describe what farms are for, who lives on farms, and what animals are commonly found on farms.
2. Ask the children if any of them have ever been to a farm before. Ask the children who have been on a farm to talk about the experience.
3. Set out the animal cutouts.
4. Hand out one animal cutout to each child.
5. Read Roger Priddy's *On the Farm* to the children.
6. Ask the children to hold up their animals when they are mentioned in the book, and to imitate the sounds their animals might make. For example, cows say "moo," pigs say "oink," ducks say "quack," and so on.
7. After reading the book, talk more with the children about the animals on the farm. Challenge the children to remember and describe to you what the animals were doing in the book, and invite the children to act out these behaviors.

TEACHER-TO-TEACHER TIPS

- If you live in an area where farms are readily available, consider taking the children on a trip to a local farm.
- Have the children remember the animals on their cutouts, set the cutouts down, and then find all the other children who had been holding similar animal cutouts by making the sounds of their animals.

Children's Books

Farm by D.K. Publishing
Moo, Cow by Salina Yoon
Oink, Piglet by Salina Yoon

SONGS

"Old Mac Donald Had a Farm"   "The Farmer in the Dell"

ASSESSMENT

Consider the following:
- Can the children identify their animals when the story mentions them?
- Do the children make the correct animal sounds?

Donna Alice Patton, Hillsboro, OH

Brett Books

LEARNING OBJECTIVES

The children will:
1. Become familiar with books by popular author and illustrator Jan Brett.
2. Learn that animals belong in different habitats (such as jungle, rainforest, and woodlands).
3. Identify specific animals by name.

Materials

3 or more books by Jan Brett

VOCABULARY

author	specific animal names	"hyena," "tapir," or
habitat	(per books selected)	"kinkajou"
illustrator	such as "badger,"	

PREPARATION

● Display books by Jan Brett in your reading area.

WHAT TO DO

1. Show the books to the children during circle or group time.
2. Explain that an author named Jan Brett likes to write and draw stories about all kinds of animals.
3. Ask the children to identify "same" and "different" qualities among the books.
4. Read a different book each day. Talk about the setting (habitat) in which the animals in the book live.
5. Review each book as indicated in the assessment (below).

ASSESSMENT

Consider the following:
● At the end of each story, point to the illustrations and ask the children to recall each animal by name.
● Can the children name the habitat where each of the following animals live: dog (house/backyard), pig (farm), bear (woods), jaguar (rainforest) and lion (African plains)?

Susan Sharkey, Fletcher Hills, CA

Children's Books

Annie and the Wild Animals by Jan Brett
The Hat by Jan Brett
Honey...Honey...Lion! by Jan Brett
The Mitten by Jan Brett
On Noah's Ark by Jan Brett
The Umbrella by Jan Brett

Earthworms

3+

LEARNING OBJECTIVES

The children will:
1. Develop counting skills.
2. Develop small motor skills.
3. Learn about earthworms and why they are important.

Materials

book about worms
pipe cleaners

VOCABULARY

burrow	discussion	fertilizer	pipe cleaner
dirt	earthworms	importance	soil

PREPARATION
- Set out enough pipe cleaners so each child will have at least 5.

WHAT TO DO
1. Read one of the books (see list) about earthworms.
2. Discuss earthworms and what they look like with the children. What do they think when they see a worm? Do they think worms are important to the soil?
3. Discuss the importance of earthworms, how they help make good fertilizer for plants, and improve the soil as they burrow through it. What do the children think they should do if they see a worm? If no one suggests that they should leave it alone, remind them to do so.
4. Have the children hold up the fingers on one hand as they count to five and repeat the numbers with you. Then have the children do this without using their fingers.
5. Ask the children to sit at the table and each line up five of the pipe cleaners in a row as if they are counting worms. They can bend and twist the pipe cleaners to make worms. Each worm can be a different shape.

ASSESSMENT
Consider the following:
- Do the children participate in the conversation about earthworms? Do the children say what they would do if they encountered an earthworm?
- Are the children able to count to five?

Shirley Anne Ramaley, Sun City, AZ

Children's Books

Diary of a Worm by Doreen Cronin
An Earthworm's Life by John Himmelman
Wiggling Worms at Work by Wendy Pfeffer
The Worm Family by Tony Johnston

Milk-Makers Match

3+

LEARNING OBJECTIVES

The children will:
1. Practice sorting by color.
2. Learn the names of colors.

Materials

The Milk Makers by
   Gail Gibbons
12 tagboard cow
   cutouts
crayons or markers

VOCABULARY

alike	cow	matching	sorting	spot
color names	different	set	splotch	

PREPARATION

- Cut out 12 cows and use crayons or markers to make cows with these colors: white with brown spots (Ayrshire), mostly brown with some white areas (Brown Swiss), reddish brown (Guernsey), light brown (Jersey), white with black splotches (Holstein).

WHAT TO DO

1. Read *The Milk Makers* by Gail Gibbons to the children several times to familiarize them with the different colors of cows.
2. Display all the cow cutouts so the children can easily see them. Ask a child to choose one cutout and identify its color: reddish brown, for example. Consider inviting each child to hold a cutout.
3. Ask another child to find a cow with a matching color. Place these two cutouts together on the rug. Ask if anyone else can add to that set. Continue until all the reddish brown cows are sorted into a set.
4. Repeat with another color until all the cows are sorted by color.
5. Mix them up and repeat, starting with a different color.

TEACHER-TO-TEACHER TIPS

- To extend this sorting activity, sort some old crayons by color and by wrappers (which crayons have wrappers still on and which do not).
- To further extend the activity, serve milk for snack, with chocolate syrup as a color-changing add-in.

Children's Books

The Farm Alphabet Book by Jane Miller
Farming by Gail Gibbons
This Is the Farmer by Nancy Tafuri

ASSESSMENT

Consider the following:
- Can the children distinguish between various colors?
- Can the children say the names of the different colors?

Susan Oldham Hill, Lakeland, FL

Mouse Count

3+

LEARNING OBJECTIVES

The children will:
1. Practice counting to 10.
2. Develop their attentive skills.

Materials

Mouse Count by
Ellen Stoll Walsh
5 mouse cutouts
masking tape
big plastic jar
(optional)

VOCABULARY

| count | mice | snake |
| escape | mouse | story |

WHAT TO DO

1. Read the story *Mouse Count* by Ellen Stoll Walsh. Ask the children questions:
   - How many mice were there?
   - How many snakes?
   - Why did the mice forget to be careful?
   - What do you think they said to each other before they fell asleep?
   - Where did the snake put them?
   - Why did he catch them?
   - How did the mice get away?
   - What is another way they could have escaped?
2. Go to the first two full pages of the book and count the mice. Then turn to the two-page illustration of mice tumbling from the jar (near the story's end) and count them again.
3. Count the mouse cutouts slowly, touching them so the children can learn to count using one-to-one correspondence. Put the mouse cutouts in the big jar, shake it, and then spill out the mice.
4. Act the story out. Make a masking-tape circle on the rug to represent the jar. Choose 10 children to be mice and one to be the snake.

TEACHER-TO-TEACHER TIP

- Count the cutouts in Spanish: *uno, dos, tres, cuatro, cinco, seis, siete, ocho, nueve, diez*. Compare the Spanish counting words with English counting words.

Children's Books

Bears on Wheels: A Bright and Early Counting Book by Stan and Jan Berenstain
Count and See by Tana Hoban
Mouse Count by Ellen Stoll Walsh

ASSESSMENT

Consider the following:
- Can the children count 10 objects in sequence? How many can they count?
- Can the children retell the story in the correct sequence?

Susan Oldham Hill, Lakeland, FL

Zoo Animals

3+

LEARNING OBJECTIVES

The children will:

1. Learn about the different kinds of zoo animals.
2. Learn that not all zoos are the same.
3. Develop large and small motor skills.
4. Develop curiosity about animals in zoos and in the wild.

Materials

books about zoos, such as *My Visit to the Zoo* by Aliki and *Going to the Zoo* by Tom Paxton

blocks

small building items, such as LEGO® blocks

small plastic animals

VOCABULARY

animal names   visit   zoo   zookeeper

PREPARATION

● Set the above items in a work area for the children.

WHAT TO DO

1. Read a zoo book or two. Ask the children if they have been to the zoo.
2. Encourage them to talk about their experiences by asking them questions:
   - What animals did you see at the zoo?
   - What are your favorite animals?
   - Do you like the zoo?
   - What else can you tell the class about the zoo?
   - Do you know that all zoos are not the same?
3. Encourage all the children to participate in the conversation.

TEACHER-TO-TEACHER TIP

● Have the children build their own zoo with the materials. They can put animals in different areas of the zoo. It is often best if the children work in small groups of two to four.

ASSESSMENT

Consider the following:

● Can the children describe what they saw when they visited the zoo?
● What animals would the children like to see when they go to the zoo again?

Shirley Anne Ramaley, Sun City, AZ

Children's Books

If Anything Ever Goes Wrong at the Zoo by Mary Jean Hendrick

A Kids' Guide to Zoo Animals by Michelle Gilders

Never, Ever Shout in a Zoo by Karma Wilson and Douglas Cushman

The Zoo Book by Jan Pfloog

4+

Folk Tale Puppet Fun:
The Little Red Hen

LEARNING OBJECTIVES

The children will:
1. Repeat simple lines given by the teacher.
2. Take turns saying their own parts.

Materials

selection of animal
   puppets (one for
   each child and
   teacher)
text of "The Little
   Red Hen"
sack or pillowcase
notepaper
pen

VOCABULARY

animal names	folktale	lazy	story
character	helpful	puppets	tale

PREPARATION

- Locate the text for the story of "The Little Red Hen" in a picture book or anthology.
- Create an outline of the story, leaving the animal names blank.
- Place the animal puppets in a sack or pillowcase.

WHAT TO DO

1. Invite the children to sit in a circle. Begin by reading the story of "The Little Red Hen."
2. Prompt the children to reach into the sack and pull out a puppet without peeking.
3. Name your own puppet as the lead character and narrate the tale (for example, The Little Brown Bunny).
4. Direct the children to add their own parts, speaking in turn from your right. Examples: "'Not I,' said the squirrel," "'Not I!' said the cow," "'Not I,' said the bear," and so on.
5. Complete the tale with applause.

Children's Books

*Folktails: Animal
Legends from Around
   the World* by
Jan Thornhill
The Giant Cabbage by
Cherie B. Stihler
*The Green Frogs:
A Korean Folktale* by
Yumo Heo

ASSESSMENT

Consider the following:
- List the children's names in a column of a writing tablet. Ask another adult to observe the activity and mark a check by the corresponding name each time a child responds with a correct line at the appropriate time.
- Are the children able to retell the story?

Susan Sharkey, Fletcher Hills, CA

Hibernation

LEARNING OBJECTIVES

The children will:
1. Develop an understanding of the word hibernation.
2. Develop their large motor skills.

Materials

picture book (from the list below)

VOCABULARY

animal names	game	hibernation
awake	habitats	kneel

WHAT TO DO

1. In an open play area, gather the children in a circle. Read the book of your choice from the list on this page, pausing as necessary to discuss and answer questions the children have.
2. Talk about hibernation: which animals hibernate, why they sleep through the winter, where they hibernate, and so on.
3. Tell the children you are going to play a game called "Hibernating Animals." Pretend you are an animal that hibernates in the winter. Tell them that when you say "awake," they should walk toward you, and when you say "hibernate" they should stop and kneel down (this game is similar to "Red Light, Green Light").
4. Have the children identify what kind of animal they are pretending to be. Let them practice walking when they hear the word "awake" and stopping and kneeling down when they hear the word "hibernate."
5. When the children are ready, have them start at one end of the room. Alternate between saying "awake" and "hibernate."
6. The first child to reach you becomes the new leader. Have the rest of the children return to the end of the room to start again. Assist the children when necessary. Repeat until all of the children have a turn to lead the group.

ASSESSMENT

Consider the following:
- Do the children understand the basic idea of hibernation?
- How well do the children follow directions while playing the game?

Kathryn Hake, Brownsville, OR

Children's Books

Arctic Lights, Arctic Nights by Debbie Miller
Bear Snores On by Karma Wilson
Old Bear by Kevin Henkes
Snug as a Big Red Bug by Frank B. Edwards
Time to Sleep by Denise Fleming
The Very Best Bed by Rebekah Raye

Hop a Rhyme

4+

LEARNING OBJECTIVES

The children will:
1. Learn rhyming words associated with the movement of animals.
2. Learn about ponds and what a lily pad is.

VOCABULARY

fly	hover	plunge	shiver
game	lily pad	quiver	wade
hop	match	rhyme	wriggle

PREPARATION

- Make several animal stick puppets (at least one per child). Laminate them and glue them to craft sticks.
- On a shower curtain, draw a pond. Draw lily pads in the pond. On each pad write a rhyming word from *In the Small, Small Pond*.

WHAT TO DO

1. Lay the shower curtain on the floor. Place animal markers face up on the lily pads with which they coordinate. For example, place dragonfly markers on the words "shiver" and "quiver."
2. Introduce the children to the concept of rhyming.
3. Read the story *In the Small, Small Pond* by Denise Fleming.
4. Give each child an animal stick puppet and challenge the child to "hop" or "fly" that animal to the lily pad with the matching animal's image on it.
5. When the children land on those lily pads, read the rhyming words on the lily pads, and then ask the children to repeat the words back to you.
6. Put the cards back down on the lily pads and ask the child to hop to the next pad with the matching animal on it, then to say both the word from the first lily pad and the word from the new lily pad. Assist the children if they are having any difficulty with this part of the activity.
7. Continue until the children say all the rhyming words associated with their animal or insect.

ASSESSMENT

Consider the following:
- Can the children find the correct lily pads?
- Can the children remember the rhyming words from one lily pad to the next?

Quazonia Quarles, Newark, DE

Materials

In the Small, Small Pond by Denise Fleming
blue shower curtain
animal markers
pictures of a
   tadpoles,
   dragonflies,
   turtles, geese,
   frogs, herons,
   and other pond
   creatures
craft sticks
black, brown, and
   green markers
glue

Children's Books

All Eyes on the Pond by Michael J. Rosen
Around the Pond: Who's Been Here? by Lindsay Barrett George
In the Tall, Tall Grass by Denise Fleming

Mixed-Up Animals

LEARNING OBJECTIVES

The children will:
1. Use creative thinking to create mixed-up animals.
2. Identify animals by individual body parts.

Materials

Cock-a-Doodle-Moo: A Mixed Up Menagerie by Keith DuQuette
1 piece of paper for each child
pictures of animals from books or magazines
crayons
glue

VOCABULARY

animal names	habitat	mixed up
bodies	head	

PREPARATION

- Photocopy pictures of animals and/or cut them out of magazines.
- Cut the animal pictures into heads and bodies.

WHAT TO DO

1. Read *Cock-a-Doodle-Moo* by Keith DuQuette to the children.
2. Discuss the concept of habitats and how animals are suited to the environments in which they live.
3. Give each child a piece of paper.
4. Each child uses one animal head and one body (see Preparation) to create a mixed-up animal.
5. Ask the children to think about where their animal would live. Have them draw and color their animal's habitat on their paper.
6. Have the children come up with a name for their animals. Help each child write the animal's name on their papers.

TEACHER-TO-TEACHER TIPS

- To add a language and literacy component to this activity, ask the children to dictate or write a sentence or two about their animal.
- Create a class book of mixed-up animals. Send the book home with one child each night to share with their family.

ASSESSMENT

Consider the following:
- Do the children choose an appropriate name for their animal?
- Do the children choose a habitat that makes sense for their animal?

Janet Hammond, Mount Laurel, NJ

Children's Books

Do Cows Eat Cake? by Michael Dahl
Mix and Match Animals by Mique Moriuchi
Not All Animals Are Blue by Beatrice Boutignon

Owls

4+

LEARNING OBJECTIVES

The children will:
1. Use puppets to develop creativity and imagination.
2. Develop social awareness.
3. Develop language skills.
4. Learn about owls.

Materials

one or two books about owls
large white tube socks
buttons
glue

VOCABULARY

eyes	hoot	nighttime	puppet	wings
fly	hunt	owls	silent	

PREPARATION

● Ask the children to bring a large white sock and two buttons to class. (Have a few extra of each in case a child forgets to bring some in.)

WHAT TO DO

1. Read one of the books about owls (see list on this page).
2. Discuss owls and how they live and eat. They sleep during the day and hunt by night with "silent wings." There are many kinds of owls. Have the children seen owls? What do they think about owls?
3. Ask the children to glue two buttons on a white sock for owl's eyes, then put their hand in the "owl" and make hooting owl sounds. Encourage them to take turns "flying" around the room with their puppets.

POEM

Five Little Owls by Shirley Anne Ramaley

Five little owls, wishing there were more, (hold up the five fingers of one hand)
One flew away and then there were four. (make flying motions with arms, then hold up four fingers)
Four little owls, sitting in a tree,
One flew back home and then there were three. (hold up three fingers)
Three little owls, feeling kind of blue,
One up and left, and then there were two. (hold up two fingers)
Two little owls, not having any fun,
One flew away and then there was one. (hold up one finger)
One little owl, sitting all alone,
He flew away and went right back home! (close hand and say, "Hoot, hoot, hoot!")

ASSESSMENT

Consider the following:
● Ask the children to tell you about owls.
● When shown pictures of various birds, can the children pick out the owls?

Children's Books

Good Night, Owl! by Pat Hutchins
Owl Moon by Jane Yolen
Owls by Gail Gibbons

Shirley Anne Ramaley, Sun City, AZ

Paws, Claws, Hands, and Feet

LEARNING OBJECTIVES

The children will:
1. Practice their large and small motor skills.
2. Learn how animals use their limbs and imitate them.

Materials

Paws, Claws, Hands, and Feet by Kimberly Hutmacher

VOCABULARY

bird	flap	jump	swim
cat	flippers	kangaroo	talons
claws	frog	paws	turtle
crawl	hands	penguin	wings
dig	hop	squirrel	
feet	imitate	stalk	

WHAT TO DO

1. After reading *Paws, Claws, Hands, and Feet* with the children, talk about how individual animals use their paws, claws, hands, and feet.
2. Ask the children to imitate the different animals. Challenge them to dig like a squirrel, waddle and swim like a penguin, crawl like a turtle, stalk like a cat, hop like a frog, jump like a kangaroo, flap wings like a bird, and so on.
3. Encourage the children to observe one another as they imitate these animals.

TEACHER-TO-TEACHER TIP

- Consider having different children imitate the actions of different animals, and then challenge the children to find the others who are imitating the same animals that they are.

ASSESSMENT

Consider the following:
- Can the children name different animals?
- Can the children show you how the animals use their paws, claws, hands, and feet?
- Can the children identify the animals in the book by name?

Kimberly Hutmacher, Illiopolis, IL

Children's Books

Paws and Claws by Erica Farber
Scarface Claw by Lynley Dodd
Whose Feet Are These? by Peg Hall

What Animals Eat

4+

LEARNING OBJECTIVES

The children will:
1. Learn the different foods animals eat.
2. Compare the differences and similarities between foods that each animal eats.

Materials

pictures of different foods that animals eat
pictures of animals
1 large sheet of paper per child
glue

VOCABULARY

berries	bugs	grain	insects	nuts	seeds
bones	eating	grass	leaves	plants	twigs

PREPARATION
- Lay out materials at the art table.

WHAT TO DO

1. Read one of the suggested books (see list on this page) and then engage the children in a discussion about what animals eat.
2. Encourage the children to go to the art table and choose a picture of one or two animals they would like to work with.
3. Have the children glue their animal to a large piece of paper and then glue pictures of the food or foods that their animal eats around the animal.

TEACHER-TO-TEACHER TIP
- Try having the children compare the foods that animals eat to foods humans eat. This can lead into an interesting discussion and a new interest in food for the children.

POEM

What Do Animals Eat? by Eileen Lucas
Did you ever wonder what animals eat, to make them big and strong?
A mixture of some twigs and leaves, and nuts and bananas.
Cows eat grass and snakes eat mice, now that sure doesn't sound nice.
But then again, dogs eat bones. I think I'll stick to rice.

ASSESSMENT

Consider the following:
- Do the children use the words "different" or "the same" when talking about the foods animals eat?
- Can the children name the foods that different animals eat?

Children's Books

Do Cows Eat Cake? by Michael Dahl
What Do Animals Eat? by Sonia Black
Whose Food Is This? by Nancy Kelly Allen

Eileen Lucas, Fort McMurray, Alberta, Canada

All About Squirrels

3+

LEARNING OBJECTIVES

The children will:

1. Learn about how squirrels look for food.
2. Sing a song together.

Materials

small resealable
  plastic bags (1 for
  each child)
plate
snack items:
  pretzels,
  crackers, fruit,
  and so on

VOCABULARY

bag	food	squirrel	trunk
collect	snack	tree	

PREPARATION

● Fill each bag with snack items.

WHAT TO DO

1. Ask half of the children to sit in a circle and the other half to sit in a straight line next to the circle to form a tree trunk. In the center of the circle place a plate.
2. At the bottom of the "tree," place the filled snack bags. Select two or three children to be squirrels.
3. While the "squirrels" gather the snack bags and place them onto the plate sing "Squirrel Snack" with the children:

Squirrel Snack by Ingelore Mix
(Tune: "Mary Had a Little Lamb")
Squirrels, squirrels come and go,
Come and go, come and go.
Squirrels, squirrels come and go all day long!

All the food that we put out, we put out,
We put out.
All the food that we put out is all gone.

4. When every bag has been collected and placed onto the plate select two or three children to hand out the bags.
5. Repeat the activity so that each child has the opportunity to be a squirrel.

ASSESSMENT

Consider the following:

● Can the children describe what kinds of foods a squirrel eats?
● Can the children recite the song from memory?

Children's Books

The Busy Little Squirrel by Nancy Tafuri
Scaredy Squirrel by Melanie Watt
Squirrels and Their Nests by Martha E. H. Rustad

Ingelore Mix, Gainesville, VA

Birds Can Fly

3+

LEARNING OBJECTIVES

The children will:
1. Develop their thinking skills and visual skills.
2. Understand that birds move by flying, and that they flap their wings to fly.

Materials

pictures of birds
that can fly
pictures of animals

VOCABULARY

bald eagle	fly	pheasant	toucan
blue jay	hawk	pigeon	wings
canary	macaw	robin	woodpecker
cardinal	parrot	snowy owl	

PREPARATION

- Make a set of flash cards with pictures of birds that can fly and other animals that cannot fly with which the children are familiar.

WHAT TO DO

1. Engage the children in a discussion about various animals. Ask the children how different animals move around in the world.
2. Focus on birds. Talk with the children about flight. Explain that most animals cannot fly because most animals do not have wings.
3. Take out the flash cards. Show the children one card at a time.
4. Ask the children to flap their arms like wings if they see a bird.
5. Tell them the name of the bird in the picture.
6. Everyone stops flapping their wings when they see an animal that doesn't fly.

Children's Books

Feathers for Lunch by
Lois Ehlert
Inch by Inch by
Leo Lionni
*Tico and the Golden
Wings* by Leo Lionni

ASSESSMENT

Consider the following:
- Can the children correctly identify the birds and flap their arms accordingly?
- Can the children name animals that do not fly and explain how those animals get around?

Jackie Wright, Enid, OK

Scratch Like a Monkey

3+

LEARNING OBJECTIVES

The children will:
1. Identify pictures of animals.
2. Name beginning sounds.
3. Learn to play a new game.

Materials

pictures of ordinary
   objects and
   animals
4 pictures of
   a monkey
tagboard
marker
glue stick
child-safe scissors

VOCABULARY

animal names	monkey	scratch
jump rope	net	vest

PREPARATION

● Create a set of picture cards to use in a flash card game. On at least four of the cards print a picture of a monkey with the words "scratch like a monkey."

WHAT TO DO

1. Shuffle all the cards together.
2. Flip through the cards one at a time. Help the children identify the pictures and name the beginning sounds.
3. When you come to a monkey card, everyone stands up and scratches like a monkey.

TEACHER-TO-TEACHER TIPS

● Instead of monkeys, you can use different animal pictures and movements—slithering snakes, hopping bunnies, swimming fish, and so on.
● With more advanced children, considering use sight words or letters of the alphabet instead of pictures.

Children's Books

Caps for Sale by
Esphyr Slobodkina
Curious George by
H. A. Rey
*Five Little Monkeys
Sitting in a Tree* by
Eileen Christelow

ASSESSMENT

Consider the following:
● Observe how the children are able to name the pictures correctly and give the correct beginning sounds.
● Can the children recognize the monkey card?

Jackie Wright, Enid, OK

Soft Strokes

3+

LEARNING OBJECTIVES

The children will:
1. Learn to show kindness to animals.
2. Match craft pieces to drops of glue.
3. Practice small motor skills.

Materials

fake fur material, with fur at least 1 ½" long

felt scraps

2 large plastic wiggle eyes per child

fabric glue

child-safe scissors

ruler

short-napped carpet piece

VOCABULARY

appreciate	fur	pet	tail
eyes	gentle	stroke	

PREPARATION

- From the fake fur material, cut long teardrop shapes at least 10" long with the widest part 3" wide. Cut one shape per child and one for you. From the felt scraps, cut semicircles about ½" wide. Cut two per child and two for you.
- Help the children assemble their fur pets. Glue two wiggle eyes at the widest end of your teardrop shape. Glue two semicircles above the eyes with the rounded ends facing toward the tail end.

WHAT TO DO

1. Talk about treating the animals we keep as pets with kindness: playing gently with them, feeding them, making sure they have water, and exercising them. To show how animals appreciate being stroked gently, bring out your fake fur pet from behind you or from your pocket.
2. Lay it on the carpet and stroke it firmly but gently. It should rise to meet your hand, as if in appreciation. Help the children make fur pets by letting them put wiggle eyes and felt semicircles on dots of glue you place on their teardrop shapes.
3. While waiting for the glue to dry, discuss how animals might protect themselves if not treated gently.

ASSESSMENT

Consider the following:
- Do the children play kindly with their fur pets?
- Do the children stroke their fur pets gently?

Children's Books

A Kids' Guide to Zoo Animals by Michelle Gilders

Never, Ever Shout in a Zoo by Karma Wilson and Douglas Cushman

The Zoo Book by Jan Pfloog

Kay Flowers, Summerfield, OH

Who Hatches from an Egg?

3+

LEARNING OBJECTIVES

The children will:
1. Learn about animals that hatch from an egg.
2. Learn a song.

Materials

at least 1 plastic egg per child
small pictures of animals to put inside the eggs

VOCABULARY

| alligator | chicken | egg | hatch | snake |
| bird | duck | fish | hunt | turtle |

PREPARATION

● Put a picture of an animal in each egg, some that hatch from an egg (alligator, fish, bird, chicken, duck, turtle, snake) and some that do not.
● Hide the eggs around the classroom for the children to find.

WHAT TO DO

1. During circle or group time, discuss how some animals hatch from eggs and others do not.
2. Invite the children to hunt around the classroom until they find an egg. When they find an egg, have them come sit down but keep their egg closed.
3. When the eggs are found and everyone is sitting down, take turns opening each egg. Discuss whether the animal hatches from an egg or not. If it does, sing this song:

What Hatches from an Egg? by Sue Fleischmann
(Tune: "Mary Had a Little Lamb")
A ____ *hatches from an egg* (sing the name of the animal you found in the egg)
From an egg, from an egg.
A ____ *hatches from an egg*
____, ____, ____! (sound animal makes, such as "quack" or "tweet")

ASSESSMENT

Consider the following:
● Invite the children to draw a picture of something that hatches from an egg to make a class book.
● Can the children name something that hatches from an egg? Use this assessment as a transition activity. Ask each child to name something that hatches from an egg. Examples include alligators, fish, birds, chickens, ducks, turtles, and snakes.

Sue Fleischmann, Sussex, WI

Children's Books

Horton Hatches the Egg by Dr. Seuss
How and Why Animals Hatch from Eggs by Elaine Pascoe
Where Do Chicks Come from? by Amy Sklansky

Animal Scenes

LEARNING OBJECTIVES

The children will:
1. Become familiar with the classification and grouping of animals.
2. Develop their small motor, word recognition, and language skills.

Materials

felt board with felt animals and felt scenes such as a zoo, a farm, or inside a house paper labels of the names of the different animals (**Note:** Consider gluing each to a piece of felt.)

VOCABULARY

farm	homes	pets	scenes	zoo
groups	live	read	words	

WHAT TO DO

1. The children can do this activity individually or in a small group. If it is a small group, have all materials ready and close by you.
2. Show a scene, and as you pick up an animal, ask the children to name it, and then ask if it would go with the scene. For example, ask the children, "Will the elephant go into the zoo?"
3. Ask the children where the word "elephant" is and have them place it next to that animal. Help the children if they have difficulty locating or identifying the word.

TEACHER-TO-TEACHER TIP

- Children love this activity and many like to do this alone or with a partner. This is a great activity to use when introducing the different animal groups.

SONG

We Live In by Eileen Lucas   (Tune: "Mary Had a Little Lamb")

The hippopotamus lives in the zoo,
in the zoo, in the zoo.
The hippopotamus lives in the zoo,
In the zoo, zoo, zoo.

My pet hamster lives in his cage,
in his cage, in his cage.
My pet hamster lives in his cage,
In his cage, cage, cage.

The little pink pig lives on the farm,
on the farm, on the farm.
The little pink pig lives on the farm,
On the farm, farm, farm.

I live in a house, in a house, in a house.
I live in a house, house, house.
That's where I live.

(Additional verses: Replace the animals with different ones in each verse.)

ASSESSMENT

Consider the following:
- Listen to the conversations to see if the children are using related words and classifying the different animal groups.
- Are the children helping each other with this activity?

Eileen Lucas, Fort McMurray, Alberta, Canada

Children's Books

A Kids' Guide to Zoo Animals by Michelle Gilders
Who's Hiding? by Saturo Onishi
The Zoo by Suzy Lee

Animal Song

4+

LEARNING OBJECTIVES

The children will:
1. Practice taking turns.
2. Learn animal sounds.
3. Increase memory skills.

Materials

VOCABULARY

animal names	noise	taking turns
favorite	sounds	writing

WHAT TO DO

1. Ask the children, one at a time, to tell you their favorite animal—only one word, such as "tiger" or "dog." Ask them to repeat this as you go around the circle.
2. Once the children can do it fairly quickly, tell them they are going to use animal sounds instead of animal names.
3. Ask what noise their animals make. These will be varied. For example, dogs can say "woof," "bow-wow," "ruff-ruff," "growl," and so on.
4. Ask the children to choose what their animals are going to say, including less vocal ones, such as fish, rabbits, and other animals. Give suggestions if necessary, such as "bubble-bubble" for fish, a high-pitched squeak for a mouse and a deep one for a rat, or "slither-slither" for a snake.
5. Go around the circle again. This time, have the children make their animal sounds in turn.
6. Suggest that the children "sing" their sounds—any way they want to—and go around again. The result should be a funny, varied, and exciting.
7. The children will love performing their animal song for a different group of children or their parents and family members on a special occasion.

TEACHER-TO-TEACHER TIP

- Extend this activity by asking the children to make up an action to accompany their pet sound, such as stroking a purring cat or cleaning whiskers.

ASSESSMENT

Consider the following:
- Ask the children which animals do not make a noise.
- Say animal names and ask the children to make the appropriate noise.
- Are the children able to wait their turn before shouting out their sound?

Children's Books

Five Little Monkeys Sitting in a Tree by Eileen Christelow
The Furry Alphabet Book by Jerry Pallotta
My Pets by Jane Brettle

Anne Adeney, Plymouth, England, United Kingdom

Animal Sounds

LEARNING OBJECTIVES

The children will:

1. Talk about animals and the sounds they make.
2. Match animal images to the animals' sounds.

Materials

tagboard
pictures of animals
computer or
    marker
pocket chart

RELATED VOCABULARY

cat	match	pig
cock-a-doodle-doo	meow	quack
cow	moo	rooster
duck	neigh	sound
horse	oink	

PREPARATION

- Create a header card labeled "Animal Sounds" for the pocket chart with the instructions to "Match the animals to the sounds they make."
- Create two sets of cards. On one set put pictures of various animals with their names. On the second set print the sounds that those animals make.

WHAT TO DO

1. At circle or group time, place the header card in the top row of a pocket chart.
2. Help the children identify each animal card as you place it in the pocket chart. Ask the children to make the sounds on the cards after you name the sounds.

ASSESSMENT

Consider the following:

- How actively do the children participate in the activity?
- Are the children able to correctly match the sound with the animal?

Jackie Wright, Enid, OK

Children's Books

Cat Goes Fiddle-i-Fee
    by Paul Galdone
The Farm Book by
    Jan Pfloog
*Spots, Feathers, and
    Curly Tails* by
    Nancy Tafuri
This Is the Farmer by
    Nancy Tafuri

Backyard Birds

4+

LEARNING OBJECTIVES

The children will:
1. Learn to look for birds in their backyards and neighborhoods.
2. Learn about birds in their area and that each area of the country is unique.

Materials

bird book or
  magazine
paper
colorful crayons
  and pencils

VOCABULARY

area	bird names	feathers	neighborhood
backyard	color	fledgling	nest

PREPARATION

- Place the paper, crayons, and pencils on the tables.

WHAT TO DO

1. Sit in a circle and show the children pictures of birds in a bird book or bird magazine.
2. Talk with the children about the birds in your area. Have the children seen birds in their backyard? Encourage them to talk about this. What colors are the birds? Have they seen any nests? Do they understand that in other neighborhoods there may be different kinds of birds?
3. Suggest that each child draw a bird.
4. Hang the pictures on the wall for everyone to see.

POEM

Little Bird by Shirley Anne Ramaley
Oh, little bird, so high in the tree! (raise arms up high)
I'm looking at you; do you see me? (point up high, then back at self)
Soon you will fly, up into the sky. (make flying motions with arms)
I want to go with you, so far and so high. (reach way up high)

Children's Books

Backyard Bird Watching for Kids: How to Attract, Feed, and Provide Homes for Birds by George H. Harrison and Kit Harrison
Feathers for Lunch by Lois Ehlert
Take a Backyard Bird Walk by Jane Kirkland

ASSESSMENT

Consider the following:
- Ask the children to tell about the birds they have seen. Do the children understand that different areas of the country, and the world, have different kinds of birds?
- Are the children able to name one or two birds that live in the neighborhood?

Shirley Anne Ramaley, Sun City, AZ

Guess the Pet

LEARNING OBJECTIVES

The children will:
1. Learn the names of various animals.
2. Begin to identify animals by their physical characteristics.

Materials

pictures of various pets

VOCABULARY

bird	fish	hamster	rabbit	whiskers
cat	fur	mouse	shell	
dog	gerbil	pet	turtle	

WHAT TO DO

1. Talk with the children about different animals that might make good pets. Ask the children if they have any pets at home.
2. Ask the children to name several animals that would not make good pets, and ask the children to describe why those animals would not make good pets.
3. Ask the children to describe various attributes of their pets, or of creatures they would like to have as pets.

4. Take out several images of different pets. Cover the images and ask the children to try and identify the pets, giving clues about the pets' attributes, and showing the children some portion of the pet, such as a dog's tail or a rabbit's ear.

TEACHER-TO-TEACHER TIP

- If they are able to do so, ask the children to give the clues for their friends to guess their pet.

Children's Books

Just Me and My Puppy by Mercer Mayer
The Perfect Pet by Margie Palatini
Pet Show by Ezra Jack Keats

ASSESSMENT

Consider the following:
- Can the children identify animals by their characteristics?
- Can the children identify animals that would not make good pets?

Sandra Ryan, Buffalo, NY

Let's Sound Out the Animals

4+

LEARNING OBJECTIVES

The children will:
1. Develop their reading skills.
2. Associate animal words with pictures.
3. Learn to sound out letters and recognize animals.

Materials

laminated pictures
of animals
clear contact paper
, or laminating
machine
scissors (adult use
only)
permanent marker

VOCABULARY

| animal | duck | penguin | snake | walrus |
| cow | part | read | sounds | zebra |

PREPARATION

- Laminate the pictures of animals that you wish to use. The animals may relate to a certain category, such as farm, zoo, or wild animals. It is good to use larger pictures, laminate them, and then cut them in half.
- Take a permanent marker and write the animal word on the two halves; for instance "cat" would have a "c" on the body and "at" on the head.

WHAT TO DO

1. Gather the children in a circle or group. Spread all the pieces of the animal pictures around the floor where all the children can see them.
2. Pick up one picture piece and ask the children to try to guess what animal it is, saying the word.
3. Choose a child to come up to find the other part of the animal by looking for both the body part and part of the word.
4. When the child finds both halves of the animal, place the animal together and sound out the animal's name with the children.

TEACHER-TO-TEACHER TIPS

- This activity can work as a matching game.
- Sometimes a lot of conversation about the animals takes place, so allow for extra time.

ASSESSMENT

Consider the following:
- Are the children able to make the letter sounds and form the animal's name?
- Can the children match the animal parts to make a whole animal?

Children's Books

African Animals ABC by
Stella Blackstone
Animal Noises by
Dawn Apperley
Punk Farm by
Jarrett J. Krosoczka

Eileen Lucas, Fort McMurray, Alberta, Canada

Match the Legs

LEARNING OBJECTIVES

The children will:
1. Develop matching skills.
2. Learn the characteristics of various animals.
3. Develop listening skills.

Materials

pictures of animals
scissors (adult use
    only)

VOCABULARY

alike	different	match	top
bottom	half	same	

PREPARATION

● Cut out or draw pictures of several different animals. Then, cut across the center of each one to separate the legs from the bodies.

WHAT TO DO

1. Hold up the top half of one animal. Then pair it with the legs of a different animal.
2. Ask the children if you've chosen the right legs.
3. Continue to try out different legs until the children agree that you have the right ones.
4. Then move on to a different animal. Keep going until all of the matches have been made.
5. Hold up the bottom half of an animal. Then ask one of the children to bring you the top half. Repeat until everyone has had a turn.
6. Show the children a matching top and bottom half. Then ask how they know that the two match.

ASSESSMENT

Consider the following:
● Can the children put the correct halves of animals together?
● Can the children identify the animals by name?

Erin Huffstetler, Maryville, TN

Children's Books

A Kids' Guide to Zoo Animals by Michelle Gilders
Mix and Match Animals by Mique Moriuchi
Not All Animals Are Blue by Beatrice Boutignon

What Are Chameleons?

LEARNING OBJECTIVES

The children will:
1. Examine a photograph of a chameleon.
2. Learn about chameleons.

Materials

photograph of
a chameleon

VOCABULARY

chameleon   desert   lizard   rainforest

WHAT TO DO

1. Pass around a
   photograph of a
   chameleon. Have the
   children describe what
   they see. What does it
   look like? What color
   is it? See if anyone
   can guess what
   kind of animal
   it is.
2. Tell the children
   they will be
   learning about
   chameleons. Explain
   that a chameleon is a type
   of lizard. It lives in many places around
   the world, including rainforests and
   deserts. It can change colors to blend
   into its surroundings.
3. Read one of the children's books
   listed to the left.

Children's Books

Chameleon, Chameleon
by Joy Cowley
*Chameleons Are Cool:
Read and Wonder* by
Martin Jenkins
Rain Forest Babies by
Kathy Darling

ASSESSMENT

Consider the following:
- Show each child photographs of a snake, an alligator, and a chameleon. Can the children identify the chameleon?
- Have each child tell you one thing she learned about chameleons.

Laura Wynkoop, San Dimas, CA

Which Animal Would You Pet?

Materials

pictures of pairs
of animals
- wolf/dog
- rattlesnake/
garden snake
- crocodile/turtle
- lion/cat
- shark/goldfish
- giraffe/horse
- weasel/mouse
- vulture/canary
- bee/caterpillar
- dolphin/hermit
crab
- bear/guinea pig
- orangutan
- rabbit
- scorpion/ant
- elephant/gerbil

Children's Books

A Kids' Guide to Zoo Animals by Michelle Gilders
Danny and the Dinosaur by Syd Hoff
Just Me and My Puppy by Mercer Mayer

LEARNING OBJECTIVES

The children will:
1. Identify animals.
2. Assess which animals they'd like to own and which ones they wouldn't.

VOCABULARY

animal names	pets	tame
habitat	responsibility	wild

WHAT TO DO

1. Ask the children if any of them have pets at home.
2. Ask the children to talk about the activities they do with their pets and the kinds of responsibilities they have.
3. Show the children the pictures of animals in pairs.
4. Ask the children which animal in each pair they would prefer to own as a pet.
5. Engage the children in a conversation about their choices. Ask some of the following questions:
   - What do you like about this animal?
   - What responsibilities would accompany owning each animal?
   - What kind of inconveniences do you think such a pet would create?
   - What fun things could you do with that animal?
   - Would the pet like living with you? Why or why not?
   - Is there a better place for it to live?

TEACHER-TO-TEACHER TIP

- Think about introducing a class pet. Low-key pets that are fascinating to observe include caterpillars and ants (in an ant farm).

ASSESSMENT

Consider the following:
- As you ask questions about each animal pair, remember that there are no right or wrong answers. Assess the children's understanding by their thoughtful answers, especially to the harder questions.
- Can the children differentiate between the animals in each pair?

Angela Hawkins, Denver, CO

Zoo Keeping

4+

LEARNING OBJECTIVES

The children will:

1. Learn to associate the sounds animals make with the name of the animals.
2. Develop their listening skills.
3. Learn to follow directions.

Materials

VOCABULARY

bird	dog	mouse	zookeeper
cat	horse	pig	
cow	lion	snake	

WHAT TO DO

1. Have the children sit in a circle.
2. Choose one child to be the zookeeper and ask her to stand in the middle of the circle.
3. Choose a few children to be different animals using the animals on the vocabulary list, or make up a list of different animals.
4. Have the children who will be the animals sit inside the circle with the zookeeper. The rest of the children form a circle around the zookeeper and the animals.
5. Once the children who will be the animals know which animal they will be, have the zookeeper begin checking on the animals by walking up to each "animal" and asking, "And what animal is in this cage today?"
6. The child should announce "I am a (name of the animal)!"
7. All the children in the circle should make the sound of the animal, along with the child in the middle of the circle who is playing the animal.
8. The zookeeper goes around to all the animals and repeats steps 6 and 7.
9. Once the zookeeper finishes tending to all the animals, repeat the activity, giving each child a turn as the zookeeper.

Children's Books

A Kids' Guide to Zoo Animals by Michelle Gilders
Never, Ever Shout in a Zoo by Karma Wilson and Douglas Cushman
Polar Bear, Polar Bear, What Do You Hear? by Bill Martin Jr.

ASSESSMENT

Consider the following:

- Are the children able to make the correct animal sounds by listening and following directions?
- Are the children able to remember which animals they are throughout the game?

Sarah Stasik, Bent Mountain, VA

Doghouse Play

3+

LEARNING OBJECTIVES

The children will:

1. Learn that an animal kept for enjoyment is called a pet.
2. Learn how to take care of a dog.
3. Discover the physical characteristics of dogs.

Materials

large cardboard
   box
scissors (adult use
   only)
paint
paintbrushes
different types of
   dog stuffed
   animals
dog beds
doghouse
collars
leashes
dog bowls
empty dog food
   containers

VOCABULARY

collar	groomer	pet
fur	leash	veterinarian

PREPARATION

- Cut holes in the cardboard box for the windows and doors (adult-only step).
- Place the box on newspaper.
- Ask the children to select the color paints they want to use to paint the doghouse and then provide the paint in paint cups with a brush in each cup.

WHAT TO DO

1. Ask the children to paint the large cardboard box.
2. Let the paint dry on the box.
3. Place the painted doghouse in an open area in the classroom.
4. Provide various types of dog stuffed animals to use in the doghouse.
5. Add some dog beds, collars, leashes, water and food bowls, and empty dog food containers.
6. Allow the children to role play caring for a dog by using the doghouse and dog items.

ASSESSMENT

Consider the following:

- Observe the children throughout the activities from painting to role-playing and record your observations.
- To assess what the children know or have learned, ask them specific questions such as, "How did you make the doghouse?" "What size dog can fit into the doghouse?" and "How do you take care of the dog?"

Children's Books

Arthur's Pet Business by
   Marc Brown
Bark, George by
   Jules Feiffer
Carl Goes Shopping by
   Alexandra Day
Clifford and His Friends
   by Norman Bridwell

Kaethe Lewandowski, Centreville, VA

Veterinarians

3+

LEARNING OBJECTIVES

The children will:

1. Learn how to care for a pet and keep the pet in good health.
2. Understand what veterinarians do.
3. Learn about the tools a veterinarian uses.

Materials

- various types of stuffed animals that represent pets
- scrubs
- stethoscopes
- basters or toy syringes
- large bandages
- splints
- prescription pads
- camera
- note pads
- pencils
- books on veterinarians

VOCABULARY

appointment	immunization	veterinarian
diet	receptionist	

PREPARATION

- Display the above materials in a large open area in the classroom.

WHAT TO DO

1. Engage the children in a discussion about what a veterinarian does or read a book (see the list on this page) to the children about veterinarians.
2. Invite a veterinarian to the classroom to discuss his job.
3. Encourage the children to role-play as the receptionist, veterinarian, and/or pet owner.
4. Take photos during this activity.

Children's Books

The Best Pets Yet by Gina Erickson
I'm Going to Be a Vet by Edith Kunhardt
Understanding Farm Animals by Ruth Thomson

ASSESSMENT

Consider the following:

- Do the children actively participate in the activity?
- Do the children indicate an understanding of what a veterinarian does?

Kaethe Lewandowski, Centreville, VA

My Tail

3+

Materials

pants and belts
(optional)
pictures of animals
with long and
short tails
masking tape
string
1 large (double
page) newspaper
sheet per child
masking tape
animal picture
book

LEARNING OBJECTIVES

The children will:
1. Learn about tails.
2. Develop their small motor skills.

VOCABULARY

balance   furry   long   short

PREPARATION

- The day before you do this activity, ask the children to wear pants with a belt the next day so they can participate in this activity.
- Consider having some spare sets of large pants with belts available for those children who have forgotten to wear pants and a belt for the day.

WHAT TO DO

1. Show pictures of animals with long and short tails. Talk about how tails help animals maintain balance while climbing trees (squirrels), swat flies (cows and horses), and jump (monkeys).
2. Give one page of newspaper to every child.
3. Ask them to roll the newspaper diagonally to form a hollow tube. To prevent the tube from unraveling, tape the end corner of the newspaper.
4. Wrap masking tape all along the tube. Tie the tail to the children's belt with a small piece of string so that the tail dangles from behind.
5. Let the children pretend to be animals and play in the classroom.

ASSESSMENT

Consider the following:
- Can the children point out an animal's tail?
- During snack time, can the children create edible tails with cooked spaghetti on animal crackers or other similar materials?
- For a family night in the classroom, ask the children to search for and bring in animals with tails in storybooks, magazines, and old newspapers they have at home.

Shyamala Shanmugasundaram, Nerul, Navi Mumbai, India

Children's Books

A Kids' Guide to Zoo Animals by Michelle Gilders
Tom's Tail by Linda M. Jennings
Whose Tail? by Sam Lloyd

Mother–Baby Match

3+

LEARNING OBJECTIVES

The children will:
1. Practice matching mother animals to their babies.
2. Learn to work with other children.

Materials

1" × 8" tagboard
    strips
stapler (adult use
    only)
mother and baby
    stickers (or small
    pictures)
pictures of mother
    and baby animals

VOCABULARY

baby	match	sticker	trade
find	mother	together	wrist

WHAT TO DO

1. Discuss the pictures of the animals and name the animals together. Ask the children to find the mothers and babies that go together.
2. Give each child a tagboard strip and a sticker. Ask her to stick the sticker on her tagboard strip.
3. Staple the bands around the children's wrists, so the bands are loose enough to slip off.
4. Ask one child to look at her wristband and find a friend with a matching band to make a mother and baby pair. Help guide the children through this process if they are having difficulty.
5. Remove the wristbands, trade with friends, and make new matches.

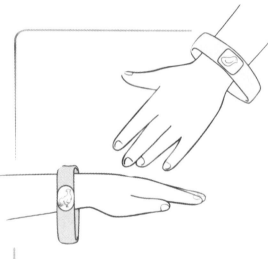

TEACHER-TO-TEACHER TIP

● To add interest to the lesson, show the children a picture of your mother.

ASSESSMENT

Consider the following:
● Give the children the mother and baby pictures to make pairs.
● Can the children identify the different animals by name?

Children's Books

Are You My Mother? by
    P. D. Eastman
A Chair for My Mother
    by Vera B. Williams
Deep in the Swamp by
    Donna M. Bateman
*The Furry Alphabet
    Book* by Jerry Pallotta
The Mother's Day Mice
    by Eve Bunting
*Have You Seen
    My Duckling?* by
    Nancy Tafuri
*Polar Bear, Polar Bear,
    What Do You Hear?* by
    Bill Martin, Jr.

Susan Oldham Hill, Lakeland, FL

Pet Dominoes

3+

LEARNING OBJECTIVES

The children will:
1. Choose an activity without teacher help.
2. Demonstrate the ability to take turns and play cooperatively.
3. Stay with an activity for a reasonable length of time to complete the game.
4. Identify and match pictures of pets.

Materials

tagboard
pet stickers

VOCABULARY

bird	domino	horse	turtle
cat	goldfish	rabbit	
dog	hamster	snake	

WHAT TO DO

1. Show the children a few completed sample pet dominoes. Explain that they will be making some dominoes themselves.
2. Set out several tagboard rectangles with center lines to resemble dominoes.
3. Show the children how to apply the pet stickers instead of dots on separate ends of the dominoes. Help those children who have difficulty with this step.
4. The children can use these dominoes to play the traditional game or they can invent some games of their own, such as matching identical pets on the dominoes.

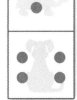

TEACHER-TO-TEACHER TIP

● Laminate the dominoes for durability.

ASSESSMENT

Consider the following:
● Do the children show an increase in their ability to use one-to-one correspondence in matching identical pets?
● Do the children display an increase in the control of small muscles in their hands as well as in hand-eye coordination?
● Do the children show improvement in their ability to play cooperatively with others?

Children's Books

The Adventures of Taxi Dog by Debra and Sal Barracca
The Best Pets Yet by Gina Erickson
Huggly, Snuggly Pets by Gwen Pascoe

Jackie Wright, Enid, OK

Zoo Escape

LEARNING OBJECTIVES

The children will:
1. Practice following directions.
2. Learn about animals that live in the zoo.

Materials

variety of zoo animals (stuffed or plastic)
cardboard box or storage tub

VOCABULARY

animal names	escape	inside	zookeeper
empty	find	zoo	

PREPARATION

- Hide the animals around the classroom before the children arrive.

WHAT TO DO

1. Ask the children to sit in a circle.
2. Place an empty box in the middle of the group; tell the children to take a look at what's inside.
3. When they declare that the box is empty, say, "Oh no, the animals must have escaped from the zoo!"
4. Ask the children to help you search the room for the escaped animals.
5. Once all of the animals have been found, call everyone back to the circle and talk about the animals in your "zoo." Discuss their body coverings, the sounds that they make, how many legs they have, and any other characteristics that make them unique.

ASSESSMENT

Consider the following:
- Ask each child to tell you something interesting about one of the zoo animals.
- Ask each child to tell you which animal is her favorite and why.

Erin Huffstetler, Maryville, TN

Children's Books

Animal Strike at the Zoo by Karma Wilson
Dear Zoo by Rod Campbell
If Anything Ever Goes Wrong at the Zoo by Mary Jean Hendrick

Many Kinds of Animals

LEARNING OBJECTIVES

The children will:

1. Demonstrate various types of movement: jumping, crawling, running, slithering, and so on.
2. Identify a variety of animals by their characteristics.

Materials

tape or CD player and instrumental music

VOCABULARY

bat	crawl	jump	run
beak	fish	kneel	scales
bird	frog	legs	trunk
butterfly	fur	monkey	wings
characteristics	hop	nectar	

WHAT TO DO

1. In an open play area, gather the children in a circle. Tell the children that they will be playing a guessing game.
2. Explain that you will tell them some details about an animal, like its color, shape, and where it lives, and that the children should guess what kind of animal it is, based on that information. For example, "I am small and green. I jump around. What am I?" The answer: frog.
3. After the children name the creature, turn on some lively music and encourage them to move around like that creature until you shut the music off.
4. Repeat the activity, this time with a different animal. Here are some sample clues:
   - I have a beak and wings. I fly around. What am I? (bird)
   - I have fins and scales. I swim around. What am I? (fish)
   - I live in the jungle and swing from trees. I eat bananas. What am I? (monkey)
   - I have wings but no feathers. I hang upside down. What am I? (bat)
   - I have a trunk and big ears. I am gray. What am I? (elephant)
   - I have a long tongue and scales. I slither on the ground. What am I? (snake)
   - I have beautiful wings. I eat nectar. What am I? (butterfly)

ASSESSMENT

Consider the following:
- Can the children identify each animal?
- Can the children mimic the animals' movements?

Kathryn Hake, Brownsville, OR

Children's Books

Brown Bear, Brown Bear, What Do You See? by Bill Martin, Jr.
A Kids' Guide to Zoo Animals by Michelle Gilders
Polar Bear, Polar Bear, What Do You Hear? by Bill Martin, Jr.

Who Am I?

5+

LEARNING OBJECTIVES

The children will:
1. Identify characteristics of specific animals.
2. Link clues together to form correct guesses.

Materials

animal pictures
figures
box or bag
masks
puppets or stuffed
   animals

VOCABULARY

clue

guess

hint

specific animal names (as
   chosen for this activity)

PREPARATION

- Collect enough pictures of animals (from magazines or printed from websites) so you have one for each child plus a few extra.

WHAT TO DO

1. Conceal the animal pictures or figures in a box or bag.
2. Explain that in this game you will call on a child to sit in the middle of the circle, then hold up a picture (figure) of an animal over her head. Remind them not to look up at the picture.
3. The child must guess the animal by asking her friends for clues. They may raise their hands and take turns telling her anything about her animal without saying the animal's name. For example, they could say, "You have long ears," "You eat carrots," or "You hop around." They should not say, "You are a rabbit."
4. Call each child to sit on the floor in front of you facing the group. Play until each child has had a turn.

TEACHER-TO-TEACHER TIP

- Impulsive children tend to call out the animal's name as soon as you show it. Allow for these mistakes by having extra pictures available. Be patient and provide some extra encouragement to master this challenge.

ASSESSMENT

Consider the following:
- List animal names used in the activity. Make note of specific clues given by each child. Evaluate the accuracy (X or O) and complexity (+ or -) of each clue.
- Complex clues extend beyond the physical appearance of the animal. "You are black" is simple and "You live on a farm" is complex.

Susan Sharkey, Fletcher Hills, CA

Children's Books

Guess Who? At the Zoo by Keith Faulkner and Daniel Howarth
Peek-a-Zoo! by Marie Torres Cimarusti and Stephanie Petersen
Wild Animals Punch-Out Masks by Anthony Rao

ABC Sort

LEARNING OBJECTIVES

The children will:

1. Develop their literacy skills.

2. Identify animals by name.

set of lowercase
    alphabet cards
set of animal
    picture-word
    cards (try to have
    at least 3 per
    letter)
bag for the picture-
    word cards

VOCABULARY

alphabet   animal names   letters   sort

List of Animal Picture–Word Cards

A: alligator, ape, antelope, anteater
B: bear, baboon, beaver
C: camel, cow, cat, cobra, capybara
D: dog, duck, deer, donkey
E: elephant, eagle, emu, eel
F: fish, frog, fox
G: goat, gorilla, goose
H: horse, hare, hippopotamus, hamster, hen
I: iguana, inchworm, ibex, ibis
J: jaguar, joey, jackal
K: kangaroo, kitten, koala
L: lion, lamb, leopard, lizard
M: monkey, mule, macaw, manatee, mink
N: needlefish, nightingale, newt

O: otter, ostrich, orangutan, opossum, owl
P: pig, penguin, parrot
Q: quail, quetzal, quokka
R: rooster, raccoon, rabbit, robin, ram
S: seal, slug, snake, sea lion, stag
T: turtle, tiger, turkey, toad
U: umbrella bird, uakari, ungulate
V: vulture, vampire bat, viper
W: walrus, wolf, wallaby, worm, water
    buffalo
X: x-ray fish, xiphosuran
Y: yak, yellow-jacket, Yorkshire terrier,
    yearling
Z: zebra, zander, zebu

WHAT TO DO

1. Display the lowercase alphabet cards on a chalk rail or rug where all the children can see them.
2. Ask a child to draw out an animal picture-word card and name the animal. Ask another child to name the initial letter on the word card, and then ask a third child to put the picture-word card by the correct alphabet card.
3. Choose a fourth child to draw out a new picture-word card and repeat the process.
4. To put away the cards when the children finish sorting them, ask a child to collect all the cards matching a certain letter.

TEACHER-TO-TEACHER TIP

● To extend the lesson, use name cards of the children's names to sort as well.

ASSESSMENT

Consider the following:

● Can the children match the animals to the letters?
● Can the children say the names of all the animals?

Children's Books

The Farm Alphabet Book by Jane Miller
The Furry Alphabet Book by Jerry Pallotta
The Icky Bug Alphabet Book by Jerry Pallotta

Susan Oldham Hill, Lakeland, FL

Action Animal Consonants 4+

LEARNING OBJECTIVES

The children will:
1. Learn consonant sounds.
2. Improve their motor skills.
3. Learn action verbs.

Materials

hazard cones or
masking tape
poster board
colored markers

VOCABULARY

| blue | bunnies | face | happy | verb |
| bounce | consonant | green | red | |

WHAT TO DO

1. Make a poster with each action verb in green, each animal in blue and each consonant in red. For example, in the sentence "Bounce with bunnies, b, b," "bounce" would be green, "bunnies" would be blue, and the letters "b, b" would be red.
2. Mark off a movement area with cones or tape. **Note**: Tell each child that he is in a bubble and if he gets too close to another child his bubble will burst.
3. Explain to the children that the green words on the poster are action verbs because you can do them around the room. Individual children can demonstrate the actions. Say the action word and the consonant sound it begins with.
4. Teach the "Action Animal Consonant Song" and encourage the children to move to it.

SONG

Action Animal Consonant Song by Kathy Stemke
(Tune: "If You're Happy and You Know It")

If you're happy and you know it,
Bounce with bunnies, b, b.
If you're happy and you know it,
Bounce with bunnies, b, b.

If you're happy and you know it,
Then your face will surely show it.
If you're happy and you know it,
Bounce with bunnies, b, b.

Children's Books

The Furry Alphabet Book by Jerry Pallotta
Guess Who? At the Zoo by Keith Faulkner and Daniel Howarth
Peek-a-Zoo! by Marie Torres Cimarusti and Stephanie Petersen

ASSESSMENT

Consider the following:
- Can the children recite the song and move appropriately?
- Can the children identify the important letters in each verse of the song?

Kathy Stemke, Mount Airy, GA

Am I Real or Make-Believe?

4+

LEARNING OBJECTIVES

The children will:

1. Recognize animals in stories and poems.
2. Determine if the animals are real or make-believe.
3. Recognize and use animal names.

Materials

Fly with Poetry, An ABC of Poetry by Avis Harley

story and poetry books

chart paper

crayons and markers

VOCABULARY

animal names	poem	talk about	untrue
discuss	story	true	

WHAT TO DO

1. Introduce or review the ideas of real and make-believe by using two different animal poems from *Fly with Poetry, An ABC of Poetry* by Avis Harley, or by reading two books about animals, one about a real animal and one about a make-believe animal.
2. Make a chart with two columns: one for real and one for make-believe animal stories and poems. When you read to the children have discussions as to why they think it is true or not true and list the name of the book or poem in the correct column.
3. Be sure to encourage discussion and allow the children the opportunity to express themselves.
4. Enjoy the stories and poems as a group.

ASSESSMENT

Consider the following:

* Have the children come up with a true story for an animal and a make-believe story. Write them on chart paper.
* Have each child draw two animal pictures, one of a real animal and one of a make-believe animal (or a real animal in a make-believe setting).

Carol Levy, Woodbury, NY

Children's Books

Engelbert the Elephant by Tom Paxton
The Hare and the Tortoise (any version)
Koala Lou by Mem Fox
Wild Baby Animals by Richard Vaughan

Crazy About Cats

4+

LEARNING OBJECTIVES

The children will:

1. Develop their literacy skills.
2. Identify the beginning sounds of the names of 16 different items.

Materials

4 pictures or
   cutouts of cats
marker
pictures of items
   with names that
   all start with the
   same consonant
   (4 sets of 4; 16
   total pictures)
pocket chart

VOCABULARY

animal names

PREPARATION

- Write a consonant letter on each cat cutout.
- Make a set of 16 picture cards, so there are four cards representing each of the four chosen letters on the cats. For example, make four cards with pictures or drawings of things that start with the letter H, such as hose, hat, heart, and hammer, or for S, make four cards with a picture or drawing of a seal, sandwich, soap, or sock on each.

WHAT TO DO

1. Place the four cats in the top row of a pocket chart to represent four columns of initial consonants.
2. Shuffle the picture cards and stack them face down.
3. In turn, have a child take a picture card, identify the corresponding initial consonant sound, and then place the card under the correct cat.
4. Continue in this manner until all of the cards are sorted.

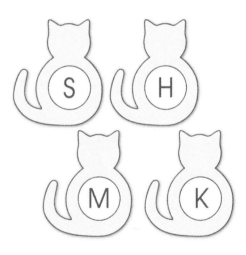

TEACHER-TO-TEACHER TIP

- Laminate the cats and picture cards for durability.

ASSESSMENT

Consider the following:

- Can the children sound out the letter on each cat?
- Can the children match the images on the other cards to the letters on the cats?

Children's Books

*All About Cats and
Kittens* by Emily Neye
Cookie's Week by
   Cindy Ward
If You See a Kitten by
   John Butler
The Kitten Book by
   Jan Pfloog
The Little Kitten by
   Judy Dunn

Jackie Wright, Enid, OK

Is It a Pet?

4+

LEARNING OBJECTIVES

The children will:

1. Experience speaking in a group.
2. Practice using complex sentences to express thoughts and feelings.
3. Practice taking turns.
4. Learn about the difference between pets and wild animals.

Materials

toy animals (plush, plastic, wooden)

VOCABULARY

difference	fierce	tame
farm animal	pets	wild animal

WHAT TO DO

1. Show the children all the animals laid out on a table or the floor.
2. Talk about the differences between wild and tame animals as well as farm animals and pets.
3. Review this after your discussion by choosing a few animals and asking the children if they are pets or not.
4. Then ask each child to pick one animal that would make a good pet and one that would not.
5. Encourage the children to take turns talking about the animals they have picked out and why they are pets or not pets. For example, "I like this rabbit because it looks cute when it wrinkles its nose. It is a pet. This tiger has very sharp teeth and it's fierce. It is not a pet."

TEACHER-TO-TEACHER TIP

- It can be quite difficult for younger children to understand exactly why they cannot keep an alligator as a pet! While you should gently guide them in the right direction, getting them to articulate their thoughts is more important in this activity.

ASSESSMENT

Consider the following:

- Is each child able to say why he picked the two animals?
- Do the children indicate an understanding of concepts such as "wild" and "tame"?

Anne Adeney, Plymouth, England, United Kingdom

Children's Books

North American Wild Animals by Colleayn O. Mastin
Pick a Pet by Diane Namm
The World of Farm Animals by Balloon Books

My Animal Book

4+

LEARNING OBJECTIVES

The children will:
1. Learn about types of animals.
2. Increase their language skills by learning new words related to animals.
3. Use their small motor skills by drawing and using scissors.
4. Build their self-esteem by creating their own books.

Materials

2 sheets of white or pale-colored construction paper per child
glue sticks
child-safe scissors
animal pictures to cut out (blank paper so children can draw their own animals)

VOCABULARY

animal names   animal words

PREPARATION

● Fold the construction paper in half sideways to make book pages.
● Stick one page inside the other.
● Staple pages together along the fold to form a book. (Let children who are able help with any part of the preparation.)

WHAT TO DO

1. Ask the children to draw four of their favorite animals.
2. Cut out the animals and glue them on blank pages.
3. The children can write or dictate the names of the animals.
4. Make a title on the front page, personalizing it for each child. For example, "Anna's Animal Book." Keep these books in the library area.

TEACHER-TO-TEACHER TIPS

● A fun variation of this activity is to let children create their own animals, such as a "kangarooster" or "bearurtle."
● Consider changing the titles of the books to things like "Anna's Book of Silly Animals."

Children's Books

101 Animal Secrets by Gilda and Melvin Berger
Amazing Animals by Betsy Franco
Animal Families by D.K. Publishing
Animals Grow and Change by Bobbie Kalman

ASSESSMENT

Consider the following:
● Have the children learned fun facts about their animals?
● Do you notice an improvement in the children's small motor skills?
● Do the children feel a sense of accomplishment by creating their own books?

Donna Alice Patton, Hillsboro, OH

My Animal Feels Like...

LEARNING OBJECTIVES

The children will:
1. Develop their small motor skills.
2. Develop their literacy skills.

Materials

premade books
different materials
    such as fur, felt,
    sandpaper, and
    cardboard
glue
writing utensils

VOCABULARY

comparing	hard	soft	touch
feel	smooth	texture	

PREPARATION

- Buy a book for each child or make books by folding sheets of paper in half, adding a piece of construction paper for the cover, stapling the papers together along the fold, and then covering the staples with duct tape.

WHAT TO DO

1. Give each child a premade book.
2. Ask the children to draw animals on each page of the book.
3. The children glue different materials on the animals to show how those animals' coats feel. They may use fur for a bear, sandpaper for an alligator or turtle, wool for a lamb, and so on.
4. Children usually have a lot to share about their books, so make time for them to read their books to others.

TEACHER-TO-TEACHER TIP

- Make sure you don't use real fur because of allergies and expense.

Children's Books

Animals Should Definitely Not Wear Clothing by Judi Barrett
Do Frogs Have Fur? by Michael Dahl
The Furry Alphabet Book by Jerry Pallotta

ASSESSMENT

Consider the following:
- Observe how the children compare the materials they use. Do they use sensory words, and do they use their early reading and writing skills?
- Do the children make real or imaginary animals? If they make imaginary animals, ask the children to tell you where the animals live, what they eat, and so on.

Eileen Lucas, Fort McMurray, Alberta, Canada

The Animal I See

5+

LEARNING OBJECTIVES

The children will:
1. Learn to use listening skills.
2. Develop creative and memory skills as they play this game.

Materials

VOCABULARY

animal   collar   fur   see

WHAT TO DO

1. Ask the children to sit in a circle.
2. Explain that they are going to imagine animals they see in the middle of the circle, but that they are going to have to work together to imagine the entire animal.
3. Walk the children through the first round of the game so they understand, then allow them to play through several rounds.
4. The first child begins the animal by saying: "The animal I see is…" They complete the sentence with the name of an animal. For example, perhaps they say, "The animal I see is a cat."
5. The next child must repeat that part, and add to it: "The animal I see is a cat with orange fur."
6. The next child repeats and adds more: "The animal I see is a cat with orange fur and a blue collar."
7. The description continues around the circle, with each child adding to the sentence for as long as the children can remember and repeat the entire sentence. Let the children help each other remember.
8. Once the children can no longer remember all of the description, have them start over with a new animal.

Children's Books

101 Animal Secrets by Gilda and Melvin Berger
Amazing Animals by Betsy Franco
Animal Families by D.K. Publishing
Understanding Farm Animals by Ruth Thomson

ASSESSMENT

Consider the following:
- Allow the children to explore their creative and memory skills further by giving them paper and crayons and allowing them to attempt to draw some of the animals they imagined together.
- How well do the children remember what the other children say?

Sarah Stasik, Bent Mountain, VA

Headband Match

LEARNING OBJECTIVES

The children will:
1. Practice matching letters and words.
2. Develop their small motor skills.

Materials

construction paper strips 3" × 24"
markers
magazines
child-safe scissors
glue or glue sticks
stapler (adult use only)

VOCABULARY

donkey   goose   horse   piglet   turkey
find   headband   match   sheep

PREPARATION

- Fold the headband strips to 1½" × 24".
- Unfold and press them flat. Below the fold, write in lowercase letters the names of farm animals: sheep, turkey, horse, donkey, goose, piglet, and so on. Also consider adding images of the animals.

WHAT TO DO

1. Ask each child to choose a farm animal. Give the children headbands and magazines, child-safe scissors, and glue sticks. Demonstrate how to find the first matching letter in a magazine, cut it out, and glue it on the headband above the fold, directly above the handwritten letter.
2. Measure the headbands to fit each child and staple them at the appropriate place.
3. Choose two children with matching headbands. Ask them to look at the other children to find someone with the same animal name. Remind the pair to look at each other's headbands to compare with the headbands of their friends. Encourage them to look at the first letter of each name.
4. Continue finding all other matches, letting each child added find the next member.

ASSESSMENT

Consider the following:
- Working with one child at a time, set out several headbands for the child to match.
- Can the children identify the animals on the headbands?

Children's Books

The Farm Alphabet Book by Jane Miller
Good Morning, Chick by Mirra Ginsburg
Over in the Meadow by Olive A. Wadsworth

Susan Oldham Hill, Lakeland, FL

My Animal Begins with... 5+

LEARNING OBJECTIVES

The children will:
1. Identify beginning letter sounds.
2. Learn to identify by sight the names of animals.

Materials

7–10 pictures of
  animals with
  different
  beginning letter
  sounds
construction paper
laminating machine
  (optional)
set of magnetic
  letters
bucket

VOCABULARY

animal names   letters   match

PREPARATION

- Glue each animal picture on a piece of construction paper, laminating them if possible.
- Select the magnetic letters that are the beginning letter for each picture (for example, "p" for pig, "d" for duck) and put them in the bucket.

WHAT TO DO

1. Lay the animal pictures in a row on the floor or on a table. Explain the activity to the children.
2. Have the first child come and pick a letter from the bucket, identify the letter, and show it to the others.
3. Next, he looks at the animal pictures, names the animal that begins with his letter and places the letter on the picture (for example, he will put the letter "h" on the picture of the horse).
4. Ask the group to say the sound of the letter and decide if the animal does begin with that letter. If so, allow the next child a turn. If not, work with the group to find the right letter.

TEACHER-TO-TEACHER TIP

- You can focus this activity by using only zoo animals, farm animals, pets, arctic animals, and so on.

ASSESSMENT

Consider the following:
- Are the children able to identify each letter and letter sound and then match them correctly to the animal picture?
- Can the children say the names of the letters?

Suzanne Maxymuk, Cherry Hill, NJ

Children's Books

Animal Action ABC by
  Karen Pandell
Animal Alphabet by
  Thea Feldman
*The Farm Alphabet
Book* by Jane Miller

Let's Have a Penguin Parade

Materials

paper
crayons and
markers
pictures or posters
of penguins
fish crackers for
snack
music

LEARNING OBJECTIVES

The children will:

1. Discuss facts about penguins.
2. Learn how to do a penguin "walk."

VOCABULARY

flippers   penguin   waddle

WHAT TO DO

1. Read to the children from a book
about penguins (see list for
suggestions), and share some facts
about penguins with the children.
2. Let the children draw pictures
about penguins.
3. Teach the children to do a penguin
waddle.
4. Let the children have a penguin
parade to some lively music.
5. Pretend to be penguins and have fish
crackers for snack.
6. Consider extending the activity by encouraging
each child to make up a story about a penguin and
act out their stories for the other children.

SONG

Penguins, Penguins by Donna Alice Patton
(Tune: "Twinkle, Twinkle, Little Star")
Penguins, penguins on parade   *Penguins, raise your flippers high*
Will you waddle in the waves?   *Waddle, waddle, wave good-bye.*

Children's Books

Penguin Parade by
Robert J. Ollason
Penguins by
Seymour Simon
Penguins at Home by
Bruce McMillan

ASSESSMENT

Consider the following:

● What have the children learned about penguins?
● What have the children learned about how penguins move?

Donna Alice Patton, Hillsboro, OH

Animals' Legs

LEARNING OBJECTIVES

The children will:
1. Develop the concepts of long and short and also learn to distinguish which animals have long or short legs.
2. Develop large motor skills.

Materials

pictures of animals
or plastic animals
with both long
and short legs
bag or box

VOCABULARY

| high | legs | low | short |
| jump | long | move | |

PREPARATION

- Place animal pictures or plastic animals either in a bag or a box.

WHAT TO DO

1. Show the children pictures of animals or the plastic animals.
2. Explain that the children should look at the legs to see if they are short or long. If the animal has short legs they get down on the floor on hands and feet and walk around like that animal. If the animal has long legs, then the children reach their hands to the sky.
3. This activity can generate a great deal of discussion about the uses of the animal legs, such as how the giraffe has long legs so that it can reach the tall trees.

POEM

If I Had by Eileen Lucas

If I had long legs like a giraffe,
I'd reach high into a tree.
But if I had short legs like a mouse,
I'd sneak into a house.

If I had short legs like a bear,
I'd love to roam and not have to care.
If I had no legs like a snake,
I'd slither and slide and in the sun I'd bake.

TEACHER-TO-TEACHER TIP

- The children may begin to make the animal sounds as the activity progresses.

Children's Books

*Four Legs Bad,
Two Legs Good* by
D. B. Johnson
*Let's Look at Animal
Legs* by Wendy Perkins
Wild Baby Animals by
Richard Vaughan

ASSESSMENT

Consider the following:
- Do the children use the words "long" and "short"? Do they understand these concepts while they look at the animals?
- Can the children remember whether an animal has long or short legs when you say that animal's name to them?

Eileen Lucas, Fort McMurray, Alberta, Canada

Sensitive Animal Toes

4+

LEARNING OBJECTIVES

The children will:
1. Develop awareness of the sensitivity and different types of animal feet.
2. Experience their own feet in a new way.

VOCABULARY

| claws | crawl | hooves | paws | smooth | toes |
| climb | feet | path | rough | texture | walk |

PREPARATION

- Gather together the various materials and arrange them into a "texture path" that is about 1' × 8'. Use alternating textures so that the children will feel smooth, rough, warm, or cool as they walk down the path.
- Be sure to cushion any rough edges, and secure the materials with thick, strong tape.

WHAT TO DO

1. Show the children animal pictures and discuss the different types of feet they see.
2. Discuss details and introduce the vocabulary. What would the animals feel as they walked or crawled along the ground, swam in water, or climbed in trees? How about animals hunting in the jungle or those burrowing underground?
3. Have the children take off their shoes and examine their own "animal toes."
4. Next, point out the different materials in the texture path. How will each one feel underfoot? Demonstrate a slow and deliberate walk down the path, describing what you sense as you go along.
5. Finally, ask the children if they want to try. Have the children line up at one end of the path, and walk through one by one. What textures are they touching as they move?

TEACHER-TO-TEACHER TIP

- If building a texture path outdoors, include more robust materials, such as brick, sand, stone, or twigs. Grass, mud, clay, and water also create interesting textures.

ASSESSMENT

Consider the following:
- Can the children identify the details of the various animals' feet?
- Can the child describe what they feel walking along the path?

Patrick Mitchell, Yagoto, Nagoya, Japan

Materials

bubble wrap
carpet squares
wood tiles
crinkly paper
plastic grass
other textured
  materials
tape
blindfold (optional)

Children's Books

Paws and Claws by
  Erica Farber
The Seals on the Bus by
  Lenny Hort
Whose Feet Are These?
  by Peg Hall

Animal Grab

LEARNING OBJECTIVES

The children will:
1. Identify animals by name.
2. Develop their large motor skills.

Materials

toy animals
bell

VOCABULARY

animal	move	sort	wild
farm	pets	water	

WHAT TO DO

1. Arrange the toy animals randomly about the floor of the classroom.
2. Ask the children to stand randomly about the classroom.
3. Ring a bell, which is the signal that the children begin to find an animal, identify it by name, and then move like that animal.
4. Observe the children as they move about, then ring the bell again, signaling the children to stop and choose a new animal.
5. When the children become adept at identifying the animals, consider challenging the children to say something they know about each animal when they pick it up.

ASSESSMENT

Consider the following:
- Can the children successfully identify the animals when you name them?
- Can the children say something about each particular animal they pick up?

Children's Books

Hello, Red Fox by Eric Carle
Hippo! No, Rhino by Jeff Newman
Polar Bear, Polar Bear, What Do You Hear? by Bill Martin, Jr.

Mary J. Murray, Mazomanie, WI

Feed the Fish

LEARNING OBJECTIVES
The children will:
1. Use their feet to move the "fish" (beanbags).
2. Coordinate their feet, back, and legs to move the "fish" over their head and into a "pond" (circle).

Materials
exercise mat
ring or hula hoop, approximately 18" in diameter (If you do not have a ring, use a circle cut out of paper. Blue paper will look more like a pond.)
4 beanbags

VOCABULARY

beanbag	hold on	over
drop	let go	press together

WHAT TO DO
1. Place the pond (hoop or paper circle) at one end on the exercise mat.
2. Ask the first child to lie down along the length of the mat, with the pond at the top of her head.
3. The child holds a beanbag between her feet, as tightly as she can. Then she slowly raises her feet up toward the ceiling, holding her legs straight, and continues on over her head, dropping the beanbag into the pond.
4. If possible, give each child three or four beanbags to try and get one beanbag into the pond.
   Note: If possible, either an adult can model the action or have one of the children model it with adult assistance. It may be necessary to help younger children at first.
5. If using paper for the pond, children can glue on pictures of fish on the pond.

TEACHER-TO-TEACHER TIPS
- If using paper, make the pond larger than 18" in diameter for children who are having difficulty and smaller for more capable groups of children.
- Use this activity again, choosing a different animal to feed into the pond, such as a frog, turtle, duck, or other pond creature.

ASSESSMENT
Consider the following:
- Are the children able to use their feet to carry the beanbags over their heads and drop them on the pond?
- Can the children count the number of beanbags they successfully dropped onto the pond?

Sandra Nagel, White Lake, MI

Children's Books

At Home in the Coral Reef by Katy Muzik
Mr. Putter & Tabby Feed the Fish by Cynthia Rylant
Touch the Art: Feed Matisse's Fish by Julie Appel and Amy Guglielmo

Animal Tails

LEARNING OBJECTIVES

The children will:
1. Become familiar with the concepts of short and long.
2. Learn about comparisons and measuring.

Materials

plastic animals with both long and short tails

VOCABULARY

climb	length	ruler	stalk
jumping	long	short	tails
leaping	measure	size	tape

WHAT TO DO

1. Place the plastic animals either in the math center or the sand and water area.
2. If in the math center, set out a measuring tape and some rulers so the children can measure the animals' tails.
3. If in the sand table, the children can compare the lengths of different animal tails. They can also talk about what each animal does such as leap, jump, stalk, or climb.

TEACHER-TO-TEACHER TIP
- Children like to extend this activity to other things in the center like measuring the walls, floors, tables, and so on.

ASSESSMENT
Consider the following:
- Observe the children to see if they are using the terms long and short to compare the animals' tails.
- Are the children using a measuring tape or a ruler to compare the sizes of the animals' tails?

Children's Books

Animal Tails by David M. Schwartz
Look What Tails Can Do by D. M. Souza
What Do You Do with a Tail Like This? by Steve Jenkins and Robin Page

Eileen Lucas, Fort McMurray, Alberta, Canada

Animal Crackers Estimation

LEARNING OBJECTIVES

The children will:

1. Learn how to estimate, count, and compare.
2. Begin to recognize each other's printed names.

Materials

clear plastic jar
small, clear plastic
cups
animal crackers
chart paper
marker

VOCABULARY

animal names	counting	less	same
compare	estimate	more	

PREPARATION

- Partially fill a plastic jar with animal crackers.

WHAT TO DO

1. Give each child a small, clear plastic cup filled with animal crackers.
2. Engage the children in a discussion about estimation.
3. Ask the children to guess how many animal crackers are in their cups.
4. On a sheet of paper, write down the children's estimations.
5. Hand out sheets of paper and markers or pencils to each child.
6. Have the children count out and eat the animal crackers in their plastic cups, making a mark on their paper for each one they eat.
7. After the children finish eating and counting their animal crackers, review with them the number of animal crackers that were in their cups, and compare those numbers to their original estimates.
8. Ask each child to guess how many animal crackers are in the jar. Record his estimate on chart paper next to his name. As a class, count the actual number of animal crackers and compare it to the estimates.

TEACHER-TO-TEACHER TIP

- Use only 10–15 animal crackers or adjust the number to the ability of the children. For older children, ask them to group the animals that are the same together. Encourage the children to name the animals as they are sorting them.

ASSESSMENT

Consider the following:

- Do the children display increasing ability in their estimation, sorting, and counting skills?
- Do they display a growing capacity to maintain concentration over time while involved in a group task?

Children's Books

Brian Wildsmith's Zoo Animals by Brian Wildsmith
Circus by Lois Ehlert
Night, Circus by Mark Corcoran

Jackie Wright, Enid, OK

Animal Photograph Match

LEARNING OBJECTIVES

The children will:
1. Match like animals.
2. Sequence numbers.
3. Think critically.

10 beanbag animal toys
10 number cards (1–10)
digital camera and paper

VOCABULARY

animal	match	order	same
beanbag	number	photograph	

PREPARATION

- Display each beanbag animal toy with a number card.
- Take a photograph of each animal "holding" a number card.
- Print the photographs on regular copy paper or photo paper. If desired, laminate the photographs or place each one inside a plastic sleeve for durability.

WHAT TO DO

1. Display the photographs down the length of the wall near the floor.
2. Set the collection of animals and number cards in a basket near the photo display.
3. Invite the children to read the numbers on the photo display, in order from 1 to 10.
4. Invite a child to set each animal beneath the matching photo.
5. Have the child place the number cards with the matching animals, as displayed in the photographs.
6. Invite the child to count from 1–10 as he "pets" each animal on display.
7. Invite the child to show his work to another classmate or the teacher then put the materials away for the next child.

Children's Books

Animal Action ABC by Karen Pandell
Animal Alphabet by Thea Feldman
Animal Babies by Bobbie Hamsa
The Animal Family Album by Tony Palazzo

ASSESSMENT

Consider the following:

- Hold the photographs in a stack on your lap. Display one photo at a time in random order. Invite a child to find the matching animal and set the matching number with the animal.
- Invite a pair of children to work together to sequence the number cards in order, set the photographs next to each matching number card, and then place the correct animal near each numeral.

Mary J. Murray, Mazomanie, WI

Biggest Animals

4+

LEARNING OBJECTIVES

The children will:
1. Learn about the size of large animals.
2. Practice making predictions and estimations.

Materials

butcher paper
crayons
markers
pencils
watercolor paints
  and paintbrushes

VOCABULARY

elephant	length	measuring	size	whale
giraffe	life-size	python	weight	width

WHAT TO DO

1. Look up the dimensions of an elephant, whale, or another large creature. In a large open space, roll out several sheets of butcher paper to the length of that creature.
   Note: Because most animals are large to young children, you might want to start with an animal like a cow or a horse. Once the children understand the process, you can do this activity with larger animals.
2. Tape these together, side by side, to create a long, wide sheet of paper.
3. Next, draw the life-size outline of that creature. Point out and label important features such as the head, eyes, mouth, tail, and so on.
4. Have the children color the creature with crayons, markers, or watercolor paint; you may want to cut off the excess white paper.
5. Now lay the creature on the gym or classroom floor.
6. Ask the children to predict how many children could stand within the creature's body. How many children could lie down head to toe? Have them test their hypotheses by counting as each child walks onto the creature one by one. Write the numbers on a board or poster.
7. Finally, you could make a running game by having the children run, one at a time, from the head end of the creature to the tail end. They may find that being timed with a stopwatch or kitchen timer adds to the excitement.
8. Repeat this with other animals.

Children's Books

Clifford and His Friends
by Norman Bridwell
Inch by Inch by
Leo Lionni
*That's Good! That's
Bad!* by Margery Cuyler

ASSESSMENT

Consider the following:
- Do the children understand that the cutout was the length of an actual animal?
- Do the children estimate how many children could fit in the creature's body?

Patrick Mitchell, Yagoto, Nagoya, Japan

Counting and Creating Kitten Paws

LEARNING OBJECTIVES

The children will:
1. Create kitten paws using scissors and glue.
2. Practice their counting skills.

Materials

pictures of kittens
construction paper
(brown and
beige)
child-safe scissors
glue

VOCABULARY

cats	count	paws
circles	kittens	purring

PREPARATION

- Precut large circles from brown paper and medium and small circles from beige paper to provide a template for the children to create paw prints.

WHAT TO DO

1. Engage the children in a discussion about kittens. Ask the children, "Where do baby kittens live?"
2. Show pictures of kittens. Introduce this art project by saying, "We are going to make kitten paws and count the paws. We can make four paws each and then we will count all the paws."
3. Show the children the templates of the paws and invite the children to cut out their own following the templates. Also help them cut out beige circles to put on the paws, so they resemble paw pads.
4. Help the children glue the medium and small circles on to each paw. Let dry.
5. With the children, count the paws they created.

ASSESSMENT

Consider the following:
- How well do the children cut out the kitten paws?
- Are the children able to count to four?

Children's Books

All About Cats and Kittens by Emily Neye
If You See a Kitten by John Butler
The Little Kitten by Judy Dunn

Lily Erlic, Victoria, British Columbia, Canada

Goldfish

LEARNING OBJECTIVES

The children will:
1. Work on their math skills.
2. Develop their small motor skills.

Materials

napkins
plastic cups
bags of goldfish
    crackers

VOCABULARY

clean   daily   fish tank   pet   water

PREPARATION

- Place items on the children's work tables. Be sure the tables are very clean.

WHAT TO DO

1. Practice counting to five with the children, then to 10. Explain the project for the day.
2. Ask the children to wash their hands before beginning.
3. Give each child a napkin and a cup that contains about 20 of the goldfish crackers.
4. Ask the children to count out five of the crackers and place them on the napkin. Then ask them to add five more.
5. Challenge the children to count to 10. Then they can eat the crackers!
6. Repeat with more crackers, or focus on specific numbers, such as seven or eight.

TEACHER-TO-TEACHER TIP

- Some children cannot eat the goldfish snacks, such as those sensitive to gluten. If you have such a child in your classroom, ask the parent or caregiver to provide an appropriate substitute.

ASSESSMENT

Consider the following:
- Can the children count to five and to 10?
- If you show the children pictures of a variety of fish, can they pick out goldfish?

Shirley Anne Ramaley, Sun City, AZ

Children's Books

The Day I Swapped My Dad for Two Goldfish by Neil Gaiman and Dave McKean
Goldfish, Let's Read About Pets by JoAnn Early Macken
Molly, the Goldfish Fairy by Daisy Meadows
My Goldfish by Stephane Barroux

Nut Hunt

LEARNING OBJECTIVES

The children will:

1. Demonstrate an ability to follow verbal instructions.
2. Demonstrate an ability to count to 10.
3. Demonstrate small motor skills by picking up cotton ball "nuts."

Materials

cotton balls
small paper bags

VOCABULARY

cache	nuts	scarce	store
food	pick up	squirrel away	

PREPARATION

● Write each child's name on a bag. Scatter cotton ball "nuts" around the room.

WHAT TO DO

1. Explain that squirrels gather nuts and store them to eat throughout the winter when food is scarce. Sometimes, squirrels don't find the nuts, and other animals eat them or they grow into trees.
2. Give each child a bag.
3. Explain that the children will be squirrels. They will each gather 10 nuts. Hold up a "nut," count "one" and put it in your bag. Once they have 10 nuts, they must store their bag in a safe place such as their cubby or under their chair.
4. Let the children explore, and assist as needed.
5. Once the children store all the nuts, take a break to read a squirrel book (see the list on this page). Sing the traditional song "Gray Squirrel" with the children.
6. Ask the children to find their nut stores. Discuss whether they found all their stores, or, like squirrels, misplaced some of them.

ASSESSMENT

Consider the following:

● Are the children able to follow the instructions?
● Are the children able to pick up the nuts and store them in the bag?
● Are the children able to count to 10?

Sue Bradford Edwards, Florissant, MO

Children's Books

The Busy Little Squirrel by Nancy Tafuri
Scaredy Squirrel by Melanie Watt
Squirrels, Furry Scurriers by Becky Olien

Shape Animals

4+

LEARNING OBJECTIVES

The children will:
1. Create animal art using common shapes.
2. Learn basic shapes.

Materials

colored construction
    paper
scissors (adult use
    only)
1 sheet of
    background
    paper (white or
    colored) for each
    child
glue
crayons and markers
    (optional)

VOCABULARY

beak	circle	oval	semicircle	tail
body	ears	rectangle	shapes	triangle

PREPARATION

● Cut a variety of shapes in a variety of sizes from the colored construction paper.

WHAT TO DO

1. Talk to the children about the different shapes they will be using to make their animals. Discuss what animal features might be represented by the shapes. For instance, a triangle could be a beak, ears, or a tail.
2. If desired, guide the children through the creation of an animal to help them visualize how animals are created from basic shapes.
3. Hand out the background paper. Have the construction paper shapes available to the children.
4. Let the children pick out the shapes they want to use.
5. Have the children glue the shapes onto the background paper to create their animals.
6. If desired, let the children draw additional features and/or backgrounds for their animals. Also, encourage the children to dictate to you a sentence about their animals.

TEACHER-TO-TEACHER TIP

● To increase the math content in this activity, provide a space for the children to indicate how many of each shape they used to create their animal.

ASSESSMENT

Consider the following:
● Are the children able to use the shapes to create an animal?
● If provided, do the children accurately count the number of shapes used?

Janet Hammond, Mount Laurel, NJ

Children's Books

The Furry Alphabet Book by Jerry Pallotta
A Kids' Guide to Zoo Animals by Michelle Gilders
Mix and Match Animals by Mique Moriuchi

Sort the Chameleons

LEARNING OBJECTIVES

The children will:
1. Identify colors.
2. Sort objects by color.
3. Practice classification skills.

Materials

12 precut
   chameleon shapes
   made from
   colored
   construction
   paper (2 red,
   3 yellow, 3 green,
   and 4 blue
   chameleons)

VOCABULARY

chameleon   color   sort

WHAT TO DO

1. Provide 12 precut chameleon shapes made
   from colored paper.
2. Ask the children to identify the
   colors of the chameleons.
3. Have each child sort the
   chameleons into groups
   according to color.
4. As an optional challenge, ask the
   children which group has the
   most chameleons. Which group
   has the fewest chameleons?
   Which groups have the same number
   of chameleons?

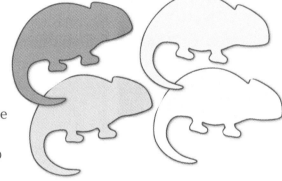

POEM
The Climbing Chameleon by Laura Wynkoop
A tiny chameleon sat under a tree.   *And was so near the sky,*
Her skin was as green as could be.   *That her skin turned as blue as the sea.*
Then she climbed very high

TEACHER-TO-TEACHER TIP
● Laminate the chameleon shapes so they last longer.

ASSESSMENT
Consider the following:
● Can the children identify the colors of the chameleons?
● Can the children sort the chameleons according to color?

Laura Wynkoop, San Dimas, CA

Children's Books

Chameleon, Chameleon
   by Joy Cowley
*Chameleons Are Cool:
Read and Wonder* by
   Martin Jenkins
Chameleon's Colors by
   Chisato Tashiro
*Counting Chameleon:
1 to 10 and Back Again!*
   by Alex Lluch
Leon the Chameleon by
   Melanie Watt
Rain Forest Babies by
   Kathy Darling

Tiger Counting

LEARNING OBJECTIVES

The children will:

1. Use counting skills to add and tally.
2. Learn about tigers.

Materials

hula hoop
several stuffed toy
tigers

VOCABULARY

stripe   tally marks   tiger

WHAT TO DO

1. Set out several stuffed toy tigers and engage the children in a discussion about tigers. Ask the children what they know about the animals, where they live, how large they are, and so on.
2. Set the hula hoop on the floor. Explain that most tigers live in captivity, and ask the children to return their tigers to the hoop.
3. As the children return the tigers to their hoop, count the number of tigers aloud with the children.
4. When all the tigers are inside the hoop, ask the children to count the total number of tigers again.

TEACHER-TO-TEACHER TIP

● For a challenge, ask the children to start with all the tigers in the hoop and then to take one tiger out of the hoop and count backwards together to introduce the concept of subtraction.

SONG

Tiger in the Forest by Donna Alice Patton
(Tune: "Oh, Where Has My Little Dog Gone")
Do you see the tiger in the forest?   *Do you hear the tiger in the forest?*
With black stripes so shiny and sleek?   *He roars if we happen to meet? Roar!*

Children's Books

Lions and Tigers and Leopards: The Big Cats by Jennifer C. Urquhart
Tigers by Jenny Markert
Tiger's Story by Harriet Blackford

ASSESSMENT

Consider the following:

● Do the children indicate an understanding of where tigers live?
● Can the children count together the number of tigers going into the hoop?

Donna Alice Patton, Hillsboro, OH

The Winning Animal

LEARNING OBJECTIVES

The children will:
1. Develop their counting skills.
2. Learn about the voting process.

Materials

paper
marker
tape
pictures of animals
chart paper
poster paint

VOCABULARY

candidate   choose   counting   favorite   vote

PREPARATION

- Ask the children to talk about their favorite animals. Choose any four animals and put their pictures or draw their outlines on a chart. Make four columns—one for each animal. Attach the chart paper to the wall.
- Create a separate voting area away from the children; place the bottle of poster paint next to the chart paper.

WHAT TO DO

1. Ask the children to vote for their favorite animal. Each child dips his finger in the poster paint and places a dot under the animal he likes the most. Each child can vote for only one animal.
2. After the children have finished voting, help them count the number of votes received by each animal candidate and to determine which animal got the most.
3. Help the children create a banner reading "Congratulations, [animal name]!" and hang it in the classroom. Children can also walk through the classroom on a victory parade for the winning animal contestant, shouting "Hip, hip hooray!"

TEACHER-TO-TEACHER TIP

- For a related family activity, children can vote for "most happy" or "funniest" relative in their families.

Children's Books

1, 2, 3 to the Zoo: A Counting Book by Eric Carle
Duck for President by Doreen Cronin
The Farm Alphabet Book by Jane Miller

ASSESSMENT

Consider the following:
- Can the children count the number of votes each animal received?
- Do the children understand the concept of voting?

Shyamala Shanmugasundaram, Nerul, Navi Mumbai, India

Animal Dance

LEARNING OBJECTIVES

The children will:
1. Practice moving like animals.
2. Improve sorting and classifying skills.
3. Improve their large motor skills.

Materials

4 sheets of 12" × 18" colored construction paper

vest, jacket, or hat with an animal patterned fabric

piece of fabric with an animal print

30 small beanbag animals

VOCABULARY

animal	move	sort	wild
farm	pets	water	

PREPARATION

- Put on the animal print garment and place the fabric swatch in the pocket.
- Print one of the following words—pets, water, wild, farm—on each sheet of paper and draw a picture to correspond to the word. Display the papers in the center of the circle.

WHAT TO DO

1. Have the children sit in a circle.
2. Give each child a beanbag animal and have the children pass their animals around the circle.
3. Walk around the circle and drop a piece of "animal fabric" in front of a child. The children stop passing their animals.
4. Invite that child to identify his animal, stand up and role-play how the animal would move about, and make any noises the animal would make (flap its wings and say "caw, caw;" slither across the floor and hiss.)
5. Invite that child to place his toy animal on the sheet of paper according to its category (pet, water animal, wild animal, farm animal) and explaining how he would classify his animal.
6. Have that child step out of the circle and spend the rest of the time imitating each "animal dance" that his classmates perform.
7. Have the children pass their animals around the circle until you drop the fabric a second time. Repeat this activity until all the animals have been sorted into groups and each child has had a turn.

Children's Books

Hello, Red Fox by Eric Carle
Hippo! No, Rhino by Jeff Newman
Polar Bear, Polar Bear, What Do You Hear? by Bill Martin

ASSESSMENT

Consider the following:
- When shown an image of an animal, can the children do an "animal dance" that replicates the creature's movements?
- Can the children identify various animals by name?

Mary J. Murray, Mazomanie, WI

Pet Owners Graph

5+

LEARNING OBJECTIVES

The children will:
1. Learn the basic concept of graphs.
2. Practice counting.
3. Exercise small motor skills.

blocks
paper
markers
large board to
   support block
   towers

VOCABULARY

| build | fewest | label | stack | tower |
| compare | graph | most | symbol | |

PREPARATION

- Ahead of time, ask the children what animals they own as pets.
- Make labels for the children's pets with pictures and names of all the different animals, including a sign for "no pets."

WHAT TO DO

1. Set up the large board and put the animal labels along the top.
2. Explain to the children that you are going to find out which sort of pet is most popular. Give each child a block.
3. Read through the labels with the children and tell them that you want them to build towers with the blocks. They must each put their block very carefully on the stack of blocks under the label showing their pet.
4. The children come up one at time and place their blocks on the appropriate towers.
5. When all of the children have added their blocks to the towers, ask each child which pet has the largest number of blocks.
6. Ask the children if they know how to prove which stack has the most blocks and which has the fewest. Hopefully they will come up with a way to compare or count the stacks of blocks. If not, guide them toward counting the blocks for each tower.
7. Explain that they have created a graph that compares information by using the symbols of the tower.

ASSESSMENT

Consider the following:
- Can the children tell you what the most popular pet is by looking at the graph?
- Can the children distinguish "higher" and "lower"?
- Ask them how to prove something has more or fewer objects.

Children's Books

Graphs by Bonnie Bader
Oh, the Pets You Can Get!: All About Our Animal Friends by Tish Rabe
The Perfect Pet by Margie Palatini

Anne Adeney, Plymouth, England, United Kingdom

Good Morning! Hello!

3+

LEARNING OBJECTIVES

The children will:
1. Develop their ability to pay attention.
2. Develop their listening skills.
3. Learn to match animals to the sounds they make.

Materials

VOCABULARY

cat	dog	good morning	horse
cow	duck	hello	

WHAT TO DO

1. Repeat the following in a sing-song chant with the children each morning, encouraging them to repeat with you. Repeating the same chant each morning for a week or more is good for young children, because the repetition will allow them to learn the words and draw them into the lesson or day with something familiar.

Quack
Quack

How does the duck say "good morning"?
Quack, quack, quack!

How does the duck say "hello"?
Quack, quack, quack!

Good morning, quack!
Hello!

2. Repeat for other animals, replacing "quack" with "moo," "neigh," "meow," and "bark."

TEACHER-TO-TEACHER TIP

● As the children become more familiar with the chant, let the children take turns improvising by adding animals they choose. Ask one or two children each morning to lead the chant and choose the animals.

ASSESSMENT

Consider the following:
● Are the children able to memorize the morning greeting?
● Can the children replace the animal in the greeting, as well as replace the sound with one appropriate for the new animal?

Sarah Stasik, Bent Mountain, VA

Children's Books

Animal Noises by Dawn Apperley
Good Morning, Chick by Mirra Ginsburg
Thump, Quack, Moo: A Whacky Adventure by Doreen Cronin

Animal Parade

3+

LEARNING OBJECTIVES

The children will:
1. Learn about the sounds and movements of various animals.
2. Discover traits that make each animal species unique.

Materials

lively music
CD player

VOCABULARY

animal names   march   parade   sound

WHAT TO DO

1. Ask the children to form a line.
2. Announce that you're going to have an animal parade.
3. Tell them that you will call out an animal and that you want them to act like that animal as they move around the room.
4. Turn on the music, and get the parade started.
5. Continue to call out animals until the music ends.

TEACHER-TO-TEACHER TIP

● To calm the group back down, make the last animal a quiet one, such as a mouse, rabbit, and so on.

Children's Books

Curious George at the Parade by H. A. Rey
Doing the Animal Bop by Jan Ormerod
Playground Day by Jennifer Merz

ASSESSMENT

Consider the following:
● Make various animal sounds (hoot, hiss, howl), and ask the children to identify which animals they belong to.
● Ask the children to name several animals that are quiet. Ask them to name several that are loud.

Erin Huffstetler, Maryville, TN

Follow That Animal

3+

LEARNING OBJECTIVES

The children will:

1. Observe and mimic movements.
2. Practice large motor skills.

Materials

VOCABULARY

copy   follow   repeat

PREPARATION

● Make sure you have a large open area in which the children can move.

WHAT TO DO

1. Have the children form a line to play this variation of "Follow the Leader."
2. The first person in line is the leader. All others are followers.
3. The leader picks an animal and begins moving like that animal around the playing area.
4. Tell the followers to "Follow that animal." The followers must copy the leader's movements, following the leader around the playing area.
5. After a minute or so, call "Stop, animals!" to tell the children to stop where they are.
6. Have the leader move to the back of the line. The next child in line is the new leader.
7. The new leader chooses an animal and begins moving. Tell the followers to "Follow that animal."
8. Continue switching leaders until time is up or everyone has had a chance to be the leader.

TEACHER-TO-TEACHER TIP

● You can have the children make the sound of the animal as well as the movement.

ASSESSMENT

Consider the following:

● As the leader, does the child move appropriately for that animal?
● As a follower, does the child follow the movements of the leader?

Janet Hammond, Mount Laurel, NJ

Children's Books

Africa Calling, Nighttime Falling by Daniel Adlerman
Over in the Jungle: A Rainforest Rhyme by Marianne Berkes
Spots, Feathers, and Curly Tails by Nancy Tafuri

Imagine That!

3+

LEARNING OBJECTIVES

The children will:
1. Match appropriate animal motions to fast or slow music.
2. Imagine how different animals might move quickly or slowly.
3. Develop their large motor control.
4. Practice listening skills.

Materials

large cleared area
such as playground,
gymnasium, or
center of room
pictures of large and
small animals
recordings of music
that suggest large or
small animals and
fast or slow
movement, such as
"Carnival of the
Animals," "Peer
Gynt Suite," "On
the Trail" from the
"Grand Canyon
Suite," portions of
the "Nutcracker
Suite," "Peter and
the Wolf," and so on

VOCABULARY

hungry   nibble   predator
movement   sleepy

PREPARATION

- Record portions of the suggested music (and any others you like) so that each selection is no longer than three minutes in length.

WHAT TO DO

1. Display pictures of different animals and choose certain children to demonstrate how they think particular animals might move.
2. Have the children think about how an animal might move if it were sleepy or hungry.
3. Put on some sample music, and encourage the children to think about what kind of animal the music reminds them of. Encourage the children to act out those movements.
4. Remind the children to listen to the different portions of music and pretend to be suitable animals that fit the music.
5. Wind things down for them by playing slower and softer music so they become slower animals or slower moving animals.

ASSESSMENT

Consider the following:
- Can the children perform appropriate movements to fast or slow music?
- Can the children continue to pretend to be animals during dramatic play?

Kay Flowers Summerfield, OH

Children's Books

Animal Hullabaloo: A Wildlife Noisy Book by Jakki Wood
The Farm Alphabet Book by Jane Miller
Never, Ever Shout in a Zoo by Karma Wilson and Douglas Cushman
Understanding Farm Animals by Ruth Thomson

Musical Animal Walk

4+

LEARNING OBJECTIVES

The children will:
1. Develop their social and emotional skills.
2. Learn to interact with adults and peers.
3. Develop large motor skills.
4. Learn about animal sounds and movements.

Materials

picture-word cards
  of animals
music of choice
tape

VOCABULARY

alligator	flamingo	macaw	rhinoceros
bear	hippopotamus	parrot	tiger
eagle	kangaroo	peacock	
elephant	lion	penguin	

WHAT TO DO

1. Talk with the children about different animals. Ask if they know what sounds the animals make. How do the animals move? Introduce types of animals that aren't necessarily typical in your area.
2. Tape animal pictures on the floor in a circle. Make sure you have enough for everyone. Start the music and ask the children to walk in a circle. When the music stops, the children stop and they must act like the animal they are standing on. How does it walk, fast or slow? What kind of sound does it make? Start music up again and when it stops they get to be a different animal. You can do this with or without eliminating any animals.
3. Vary the game by making two sets of each animal. When the music stops, the children find the other person with the same animal just by listening to the sounds and watching the movements.

TEACHER-TO-TEACHER TIP

- To extend the children's learning, take them on a trip to your local zoo.

ASSESSMENT

Consider the following:
- Are the children able to act out the animals while maintaining self-control?
- Can the children indicate the animals that make particular noises?

Rebecca Espanola, Panama City Beach, FL

Children's Books

Brown Bear, Brown Bear, What Do You See? by Bill Martin Jr.
Panda Bear, Panda Bear, What Do You See? by Bill Martin Jr.
Polar Bear, Polar Bear, What Do You Hear? by Bill Martin Jr.

Musical Farm Animals

LEARNING OBJECTIVES

The children will:
1. Follow directions.
2. Match farm animals to their babies.

Materials

large picture cards
   of farm animals
   and baby farm
   animals
music

VOCABULARY

calf	cow	duckling	hen	lamb	puppy
cat	dog	farm	horse	pig	sheep
chick	duck	foal	kitten	piglet	

PREPARATION

● Set up chairs in musical chairs formation.

WHAT TO DO

1. Hold up each picture and have the children identify the animal. Have the children take turns matching animals to their babies.
2. Tape a baby animal picture to each chair. Give each child a picture of a mother farm animal.
3. Have the children walk around the chairs as you play music. When the music stops, children quickly find their matching baby animal and sit down.
4. Have each child name their animal and their baby animal.
5. Give the children different mother animals and play again.

SONGS

Sing the following with the children: "The Farmer in the Dell," "Old MacDonald Had a Farm," and "Mary Had a Little Lamb."

TEACHER-TO-TEACHER TIP

● If your group is very large, play with half the group at a time.

ASSESSMENT

Consider the following:
● Can the children name the various farm animals?
● Can the children match the farm animals to their babies?

Sandra Ryan, Buffalo, NY

Children's Books

Animal Babies on the Farm by Editors of Kingfisher
Big Red Barn by Margaret Wise Brown
The New Baby Calf by Edith Newlin Chase

Nocturnal Nap Time

3+

LEARNING OBJECTIVES

The children will:
1. Learn about nocturnal animals.
2. Learn how to mimic other creatures.

Materials

VOCABULARY

bats   fox   nocturnal   owl

WHAT TO DO

1. Explain to the children what nocturnal animals are. Read books about nocturnal animals (see the list on this page) and then engage the children in a discussion about nocturnal animals.
2. Have the children pick which nocturnal animal they are going to pretend to be during nap time.
3. When it is time to rest, children can lie on their mats and mimic the animals of their choice through body position. For example, children who pick foxes could rest curled up, and those who pick lions could lie on their backs.
4. Additionally, children can use their imaginations and decide the best way for their chosen animal to sleep.

ASSESSMENT

Consider the following:
- Do the children understand what "nocturnal" means?
- Can the children explain why a creature might be nocturnal?

Monica Shaughnessy, Katy, TX

Children's Books

Bear Snores On by Karma Wilson
Night Creatures by Scholastic
Snug as a Big Red Bug by Frank B. Edwards

Animal Classification

LEARNING OBJECTIVES

The children will:
1. Learn about the different animals in the world and the different areas that they live in.
2. Learn how to sort animals into different categories.

Materials

nature magazines and coloring books
child-safe scissors
paper
glue

VOCABULARY

animals	forest	ocean
farm	jungle	pets

PREPARATION

- Ahead of time, draw columns on a piece of paper and label the columns "Jungle," "Farm," "Forest," and "Pets." Add an image indicative of each term at the top of the appropriate column. Make one for each child. Place the other items listed for the lesson in the science and nature center.

WHAT TO DO

1. Engage the children in a discussion about the different animals in the world. Discuss how there are animals that live in the jungle, on a farm, in the forest, and other animals that they may have as pets.
2. At the end of the discussion, set out the magazines and coloring books.
3. Explain to the children that they will be looking for animals that they just talked about.
4. After they find and cut out their pictures, give each child one of the papers you prepared for them.
5. Explain to them that they will match the different animals to where they live. Show the children how to do this on their papers.
6. Show them a picture of an elephant and ask them where the elephant lives. Once they figure it out, they glue the picture in that column of their paper. **Note**: Help the children who need a bit of guidance.

ASSESSMENT

Consider the following:
- Do the children understand that certain creatures only live in particular habitats?
- Can the children sort the animals into the correct habitats?

Children's Books

Animal Hullabaloo: A Wildlife Noisy Book by Jakki Wood
The Day Jimmy's Boa Ate the Wash by Trinkle Hakes Noble
The Farm Alphabet Book by Jane Miller
Forest Life by Barbara Taylor

Sherri Lawrence, Louisville, KY

Animal Safari

4+

LEARNING OBJECTIVES

The children will:
1. Identify various animals.
2. Experience role playing.
3. Improve their oral language skills.

Materials

stuffed toy animals
   or photographs
   or pictures of sets
   of animals
blank paper
   booklets
pictures of animals
   from magazines
   or clip art
child-safe scissors
glue sticks
animal stickers

VOCABULARY

animals	look	search
binoculars	safari	

PREPARATION

- Display the pictures of animals in various locations outside of your school (on a tree trunk, on the monkey bars, in a bush, on a fence, and so on).

WHAT TO DO

1. Explain the meaning of the word "safari:" an expedition, trip, or search.
2. Have the children line up and follow you outdoors.
3. Search for and identify real animals in your school yard (squirrels, birds, and so on) or the toy animals on display.
4. Upon returning to the classroom, invite the children to make an animal keepsake book of their own.
5. Help the children cut and paste pictures of animals into a blank paper booklet.
6. Encourage the children to "read" the animal book aloud to one another as they talk about the fun safari adventure.

Children's Books

*Animal Babies on
the Farm* by
Editors of Kingfisher
*Animal Hullabaloo: A
Wildlife Noisy Book* by
Jakki Wood
*The Farm Alphabet
Book* by Jane Miller
*Understanding
Farm Animals* by
Ruth Thomson

ASSESSMENT

Consider the following:
- Display the animals in select places of the classroom. Can the children identify these animals?
- Attach an assortment of animal stickers or pictures to a sheet of chart paper. Provide a child with a pointer. Invite the child to teach you all he knows about each animal on the chart.

Mary J. Murray, Mazomanie, WI

Whose Feet Are These?

4+

LEARNING OBJECTIVES

The children will:
1. Match animal tracks to the correct animal.
2. Match animal names to the correct animal.

Materials

stiff cardboard or
  poster board
large permanent
  markers
ruler
child-safe scissors
books on animals
  and their tracks

VOCABULARY

| animal names | different | footprints | pairs | similar |
| claws | feet | match | retract | tracks |

PREPARATION

- Cut cardboard or poster board into 5" x 6" rectangles.
- Reproduce pictures of both animals and their tracks.
- Glue these onto the cardboard rectangles to make matching pairs.
- Write the animal names in capital letters on separate rectangles.

WHAT TO DO

1. Have the children look at their feet, then look at your feet to see the differences in size or shoe tread. Tell them that if they walked in the snow or the mud, they could probably figure out who made the footprints. Animals make different footprints, called tracks.
2. From books or the cards you have made, show the children the tracks, the animal that made the track, and the printed name of the animal.
3. Point out similarities and differences. For example, dog and cat prints look somewhat alike, but on a dog's tracks you can see the tips of their claws because they don't retract them like cats do.
4. Note that certain animals' names start with the same letter as some of the children's names. For example, "opossum" starts with the same letter as Olivia.
5. After a few days, the children should be able to match the tracks to the correct animal and begin to identify the animals' names by recognizing the same letters in their names and the names of their classmates.

Children's Books

Paws and Claws by
Theresa Greenaway
Scarface Claw by
Lynley Dodd
Whose Feet Are These?
by Peg Hall

ASSESSMENT

Consider the following:
- Are the children able to successfully match tracks to the animal that made them?
- Do the children show interest in tracks they see outdoors?
- Are the children able to begin matching letters and beginning sounds to animal names?

Kay Flowers, Summerfield, OH

Feathers, Fur, or Scales?

4+

LEARNING OBJECTIVES

The children will:
1. Learn about different kinds of animal body coverings.
2. Discover that animals can be sorted into groups according to their body covering.

Materials

assortment of animal toys, photos, blocks and/or puppets
5 large boxes
7 labels or tags
samples of a piece of fur, some sloughed snake skin and a feather, or taxidermy specimens of a mammal, reptile, bird, and fish (optional)

VOCABULARY

| birds | fish | mammals | scales |
| feathers | fur | reptiles | |

PREPARATION

- Make the following labels or tags: "scales," "fur," "feathers," "mammals," "reptiles," "fish," and "birds."
- Place the "scales," "fur," and "feathers" labels on three boxes. Set aside the remaining two boxes.

WHAT TO DO

1. Discuss what scales, fur, and feathers are; what they feel like; and what they are used for (such as protection, warmth, camouflage, and flight). Pass around the taxidermy specimens, if available.
2. Have the children sort the various animal toys, photos, and so on according to their body covering into the three boxes: "scales," "fur," and "feathers."
3. As a group, look at and discuss the kinds of animals in each box. What else do the animals in each box have in common? Add new labels to two of the boxes—animals with feathers receive the label "birds"; animals with fur receive the label "mammals."
4. Note that two different types of animals are in the "scales" box—fish and reptiles.
5. Give the two remaining boxes "fish" and "reptile" labels, and sort the animals in the "scales" box accordingly.

ASSESSMENT

Consider the following:
- Can the children name the different kinds of body coverings that animals have?
- Are the children able to classify various animals based on their characteristics?

Julie Murphy, Reservoir, Victoria, Australia

Children's Books

Bird by David Burnie
Mammals by D.K. Publishing
Snakes Slither and Hiss by D.K. Publishing

Grows Back?

5+

LEARNING OBJECTIVES

The children will:
1. Learn about the life cycles of various animals.
2. Learn that certain animals can regrow body parts.

Materials

pictures of moose, starfish, snakes, locusts, or any animal growing out of skins, teeth, horns, tentacles, and so on

VOCABULARY

horns   regenerate
life cycle   stages
prefix "re" (to begin again)   tentacles
recreate

WHAT TO DO

1. Ask the children if they know any animals with body parts that fall off and grow back during their life cycle.
2. Ask if they know if any part of their bodies grow back during their life cycle (eyelashes, teeth, skin, hair).
3. Explain how the same happens with animals in different ways. Show pictures: A moose loses its antlers each year. Starfish can lose a tentacle and grow it back. Snakes get bigger and must grow out their skin.
4. Explain the life cycle as the different parts of life, like being a baby, then turning into an older child, then an adult, and finally an older person.
5. Encourage the children to imagine and verbalize what other animals do during their life cycles.

TEACHER-TO-TEACHER TIP

- Many wonderful images of these creatures are available online. Show them to the children before and after this activity for the greatest impact.

ASSESSMENT

Consider the following:
- Can the children name two animals and the body parts they regrow?
- Do the children understand that most animals do not regrow body parts?

Children's Books

Chameleon, Chameleon by Joy Cowley
Moose and Magpie by Bettina Restrepo
The Worm Family by Tony Johnston

Bettina Williford, Frisco, TX

Safari Binoculars

4+

LEARNING OBJECTIVES

The children will:
1. Develop their small motor skills.
2. Learn about animals on safari.

Materials

cardboard tubes
child-safe scissors
markers
tape
string
hole punch (adult
   use only)
toy animals
   commonly found
   on a safari

VOCABULARY

binoculars	monkey	tiger
lion	safari	

PREPARATION

* Make a set of safari binoculars for yourself prior to this activity as an example to show the children.

WHAT TO DO

1. Engage the children in a discussion about safaris. Talk about the different animals the children might see on a safari.
2. Set out the various materials. Show the children your binoculars. Explain that on safaris, people typically use binoculars to see the animals because it is difficult to get close enough to see them clearly.
3. Help the children cut the tubes and tape their binoculars together. Encourage the children to decorate their binoculars any way they wish.
4. Help the children punch holes in their binoculars and run a length of string through the holes.
5. Set out the toy animals and invite the children to watch them from afar. Challenge the children to describe the animals they see quietly, so as not to scare the animals off.

MASKING TAPE

LOOK THROUGH HERE

Children's Books

Animal Babies on the Farm by Editors of Kingfisher
Animal Hullabaloo: A Wildlife Noisy Book by Jakki Wood
The Farm Alphabet Book by Jane Miller
Understanding Farm Animals by Ruth Thomson

ASSESSMENT

Consider the following:
* Do the children have any difficulty making their binoculars?
* Can the children name the animals they saw on their safari?

Mary J. Murray, Mazomanie, WI

Animal Chips and Salsa

3+

LEARNING OBJECTIVES

The children will:
1. Practice animal identification.
2. Develop their small motor skills.
3. Improve their ability to follow directions.

Materials

animal-shaped
    cookie cutters
cookie sheet
flour tortillas
salsa
cooking spray
oven (for adult
    use only)

VOCABULARY

amphibian	cow	lion	sheep
bear	giraffe	mammal	zebra
bird	horse	reptile	

PREPARATION
- Preheat oven to 350 degrees.

WHAT TO DO
1. Give each child a large flour tortilla and a variety of animal cookie-cutter shapes. Help those children who have difficulty with this step.
2. Ask them to cut out different animal shapes, identifying the animals as they go. If they already know their animal names well, challenge them to classify the animals as reptiles, amphibians, birds, or mammals.

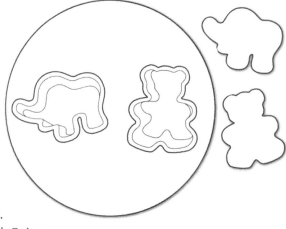

3. Lightly coat a cookie sheet with the cooking spray and place a single layer of animal-shaped tortillas onto the sheet. Bake for 5–7 minutes. Let cool. Enjoy with a little salsa!

ASSESSMENT
Consider the following:
- Can the children name the animal shapes of their tortillas?
- Can the children classify the animals into reptiles, amphibians, birds, or mammals?

Children's Books

Animal Boogie by
Debbie Harter
*Eric Carle's Animals,
Animals* compiled by
Laura Whipple
My Big Animal Book by
Roger Priddy

Kimberly Hutmacher, Illiopolis, IL

Animal Trail Mix

3+

LEARNING OBJECTIVES

The children will:
1. Practice measuring.
2. Learn about food preparation.
3. Identify animals.

VOCABULARY

animals   bowl   count   crackers   eat   measure   snacks   stir

PREPARATION

- Write the recipe for Animal Trail Mix on a piece of chart paper. Incorporate pictures when possible next to or in place of the words on the recipe.
- Use this recipe on this page or create your own:

RECIPE

Animal Trail Mix

2 tablespoons of whale-shaped crackers
⅛ cup animal-shaped fruit snacks
6 animal crackers
¼ cup animal-shaped cereal

- Measure and count out the ingredients listed above. Place in a cup or bowl. Stir. Enjoy.

WHAT TO DO

1. Display the recipe and read it aloud to the children.
2. Invite small groups of children to wash their hands and then come forward to prepare their Animal Trail Mix snack.
3. Have the children count out crackers and measure the cereal and other ingredients. Help those children who are not able to count or measure on their own or pair those children with other children who can count and measure.
4. Guide the children as they stir their trail mix, then set it at their place at the snack table.
5. Once all the children have prepared their snack mix, have them take their seats at the table.
6. Encourage the children to talk quietly at their tables, as they name the various animals before they eat them.

ASSESSMENT

Consider the following:
- Can the children measure the correct amount of ingredients to go in the recipe?
- Do the children indicate a preference for certain foods in the trail mix?

Mary J. Murray, Mazomanie, WI

Materials

4 or more different types of animal-shaped foods such as whale-shaped crackers, teddy bear crackers, plain animal crackers, iced animal crackers, and so on
chart paper
marker
measuring spoons
plastic cups or bowls

Children's Books

Bears on Wheels: A Bright and Early Counting Book by Stan and Jan Berenstain
The Chicken on the Farm by Jennifer Coldrey
Count and See by Tana Hoban
Living in a Rainforest by Patricia Whitehouse

Milk Comes from Cows

3+

LEARNING OBJECTIVES

The children will:
1. Identify foods made from milk.
2. Taste foods made from milk.

Materials

cottage cheese
small paper cups
plastic spoons
milk
drinking cups
cheese slices (any variety)
child-size yogurt cups

VOCABULARY

cheese	cow	yogurt
cottage cheese	milk	

PREPARATION
- Spoon a small amount of cottage cheese into some paper cups.
- Add a plastic spoon to each cup of cottage cheese.
- Fill other cups with milk.

WHAT TO DO
1. Ask the children where milk comes from. Then ask them what foods are made from milk. See how many different dairy foods the children can name. Help them brainstorm, if needed.
2. Tell the children that they will be tasting foods made from milk. Offer cheese slices, yogurt, and cottage cheese. Provide each child with a cup of milk.

SONG
Sing "This Is the Way We Milk the Cows," sung to the tune of "Here We Go 'Round the Mulberry Bush" with the children.

TEACHER-TO-TEACHER TIPS
- Make sure that none of the children have milk allergies before offering dairy foods.
- To make the cheese slices more fun, provide cow-shaped cookie cutters and have the children cut cow shapes from their cheese slices.

Children's Books

From Grass to Milk by Stacy Taus-Bolstad
Milk: From Cow to Carton by Aliki
The Milk Makers by Gail Gibbons

ASSESSMENT
Consider the following:
- Can the children identify the foods that they tasted?
- Show the children pictures of different foods including apples, yogurt, carrots, and cheese. Can they pick out the foods that are made from milk?

Laura Wynkoop, San Dimas, CA

Fish Faces

LEARNING OBJECTIVES

The children will:
1. Learn to recognize facial features.
2. Creatively produce an individual fish face.
3. Practice following instructions.

Materials

canned tuna
mayonnaise
cucumber
foods to decorate
   the fish faces,
   such as red
   pepper, mild
   olives, corn,
   raisins, cheese,
   carrots, and
   so on
bread

VOCABULARY

eyes   food names   mouth   scales

PREPARATION

- Find pictures or drawings of a fish seen head on.
- Drain tuna and mix with mayonnaise.
- Cut cucumber into thin slices, then slice into two.
- Cut other foods into appropriate shapes, such as curved pieces of red pepper for mouth.
- Spoon a small quantity of tuna onto each piece of bread or toast in a circular mound.

WHAT TO DO

1. Show the children pictures of fish.
2. Ask the children what features a fish face would have.
3. Show them your sample fish face and get them to identify the features.
4. Give each child the tuna circle on bread or toast.
5. Encourage the children to make fish faces, using cucumber to make scales around the mound of tuna. Suggest making eyes with cheese circles and raisins or olives slices, and a mouth with pepper slices and corn teeth.
6. Ask them to make a face on their fish with the food ingredients available.
7. Eat the fish faces at snack time.

TEACHER-TO-TEACHER TIP

- Older children may be able to do much of the preparation too.

Children's Books

Animal Faces by Akira Satoh and Kyoko Toda
Pet Fish by Robin Nelson
What Is a Fish? by Bobbie Kalman and Allison Larin

ASSESSMENT

Consider the following:
- Can the children recognize what facial features should not appear on their fish face, such as a nose and eyebrows?
- Can the children create a recognizable fish face with the ingredients?

Anne Adeney, Plymouth, England, UK

Rabbit Food

4+

LEARNING OBJECTIVES

The children will:

1. Learn at least two things that rabbits eat.
2. Develop their small motor skills.

Materials

stuffed rabbits of
various sizes
apples
carrots
celery
plastic picnic knives
small bowls
paper towels

Children's Books

Duck! Rabbit! by
Amy Krouse Rosenthal
and Tom Lichtenheld
The Little Rabbit by
Judy Dunn
*Little Rabbit's Loose
Tooth* by Lucy Bate and
Diane De Groat
My Friend Rabbit by
Eric Rohmann
*Peter Rabbit's Giant
Storybook* by
Beatrix Potter
Rabbits and Raindrops
by Jim Arnosky
The Velveteen Rabbit by
Margery Williams and
William Nicholson
*Zomo the Rabbit:
A Trickster Tale from
West Africa* by
Gerald McDermott

VOCABULARY

apple   carrot   celery   cut   rabbit   salad

WHAT TO DO

1. Invite each child to bring a stuffed rabbit to school. Have extra stuffed rabbits available for those who do not own one.
2. Invite the children to create a salad for their rabbit. Discuss the things a rabbit might like to eat.
3. Offer apples, carrots, and celery for the children to cut up. Place small bowls, plastic picnic knives for cutting, and paper towels in the middle of a low table.
4. Assist the children in cutting up the food with the plastic knives.
5. As the children work, discuss the choices they have made. Ask open-ended questions and allow the children enough time to answer.
6. Talk about what other animals would eat this salad. A turtle? How about an alligator?
7. Also discuss other foods rabbits might eat that people do not. What about clover and grass? What animals eat those?
8. Enjoy your "rabbit food" together.

TEACHER-TO-TEACHER TIP

- Cutting with a plastic knife can be difficult for some children. To allow the children to experience success, blanch the apples and carrots before offering them to be cut. This gentle cooking will soften the food somewhat and make it easier to cut without affecting the flavor.

ASSESSMENT

Consider the following:

- Show the children photos of various fruits and vegetables and ask them to sort them into piles indicating which one rabbits will eat and which ones rabbits will not eat.
- As the children cut the fruits and vegetables, observe closely to see who manipulates the tools easily and who needs extra help.

Virginia Jean Herrod, Columbia, SC

"Bow-Wow," Said the Dog

3+

LEARNING OBJECTIVES

The children will:

1. Express themselves creatively, imitating animals.
2. Learn animal sounds.
3. Learn turn-taking and dramatic techniques.

Materials

masks will enhance the performance, but they are optional

VOCABULARY

bow-wow	cuckoo	mew	tweet
caw	grunt	quack	
crow	hog	squeak	

PREPARATION

● Make masks, if desired.

WHAT TO DO

1. If they do not already know it, teach the children the popular nursery rhyme "Bow-Wow Said the Dog":

"Bow-Wow," Said the Dog

"Bow-Wow," said the dog.   *"Tu-whu," said the owl.*
"Meow, meow," said the cat.   *"Caw, caw," said the crow.*
"Grunt, grunt," said the hog.   *"Quack, quack," said the duck.*
And "squeak," said the rat.   *And "moo," said the cow.*

2. Divide the children evenly into animal groups and ask them to practice their sounds. Then repeat the rhyme, asking each animal group to make its sound.
3. Consider doing this rhyme in a variety of ways:
   ● Recite the rhyme yourself, and have the children only say their animals' sounds.
   ● Ask each group to say its line only, with all of the children saying the final two lines.
   ● Challenge each group to make up a silent action that the groups perform rather than making their animals' sounds.

ASSESSMENT

Consider the following:

● Can the children match the sounds and animals correctly?
● Can the children add their sound at the appropriate time?
● Do the children make up appropriate actions for the animals?

Anne Adeney, Plymouth, England, United Kingdom

Children's Books

Cuckoo: A Mexican Folktale by Lois Ehlert
Do You Have My Quack? A Book of Animal Sounds by Keith Faulkner
A Kids' Guide to Zoo Animals by Michelle Gilders
Whose Feet Are These? by Peg Hall

Five Little Ducks

3+

LEARNING OBJECTIVES

The children will:

1. Participate in saying the rhyme.
2. Take turns being the lead duck and the following ducks.

Materials

recording of the
song "Five Little
Ducks"
tape
feathers

VOCABULARY

big	follow	medium	small
first	leader	second	waddle

WHAT TO DO

1. Introduce the popular song "Five Little Ducks" to the children. When you sing the song the first time, show the children that the fingers and thumb on one hand can represent the five ducks.
2. The second time you play the song, the children will act it out.
3. Before you play the song again, pick one child to be the lead duck. This child will wear a feather taped to the back of her shirt. Tape a feather on her back.
4. Choose four others to line up behind the first duck.
5. The group sings the song as the four children follow the lead duck around the room. When the song ends, tape the feather on the back of the second child. The first child then sits down and chooses another child to be the new fifth duck.
6. Repeat this until all the children cycle through the group of five ducks, moving from fifth duck to first duck.
7. Encourage all the children to help sing the song. Encourage the children being ducks to waddle as they walk.

MORE TO DO

● Incorporate a "feelings" activity by talking as a group about how it feels to be the lead duck as opposed to one of the following ducks, as well as how it feels to be a watcher or singer.

ASSESSMENT

Consider the following:

● Do the children learn the song well enough to sing along?
● How well does each child take turns as a singer, leader, follower, and so on?

Sandra Nagel, White Lake, MI

Children's Books

10 Little Rubber Ducks
by Eric Carle
Ducks Don't Get Wet
by Augusta Goldin
Five Little Ducks by
Raffi
The Little Duck by
Judy Dunn

Hickery, Tickery, Trick

3+

LEARNING OBJECTIVES

The children will:

1. Listen with understanding and respond with an appropriate word, stick puppet, and action.
2. Develop number recognition, counting, and one-to-one correspondence skills.
3. Coordinate movements to perform complex tasks.

Materials

pictures of animals
tape
tongue depressors
    or popsicle sticks
picture of a
    grandfather
    clock, laminated
copy of the song for
    the teacher or
    words and
    pictures to put in
    a pocket chart

VOCABULARY

above   below   jump   left side   middle   right side

PREPARATION

● Copy and tape animal pictures to sticks.
● Laminate a picture of a grandfather clock.
● Prepare a chart with the words to the song, or prepare words and animal pictures for a pocket chart.

WHAT TO DO

1. Teach the children the following song, and then sing it together. Tell the children that the animals will do tricks to fool them. Have the children act out the movements matching the words. Use a variety of stick animals. Change the animals after each verse.

   Hickory, Tickery, Trick by Carol Hupp
   (Tune: "Hickory, Dickory, Dock")
   Hickory, tickery, trick,
   A [cow, horse, pig, deer, wolf] *ran* [up, below, right, left, through] *the clock.*
       (child moves the stick puppet to correct position)
   The clock struck [9, 2, 6, or any number], (puppet jumps x times as children
       count)
   And the cow ran down.
   Hickory, tickery, trick.

2. End with a Simon Says-type game to try to trick the children. For example, say, "Simon Says the cow is in the middle of the clock. Simon says the cow is below the clock."

Children's Books

10 Little Rubber Ducks
    by Eric Carle
Fifteen Animals by
    Sandra Boynton
*There's a Frog in My
    Throat!* by Loreen
Leedy and Pat Street

ASSESSMENT

Consider the following:

● Do the children indicate an understanding of the position words?
● Can the children substitute animals and actions without difficulty?

Carol Hupp, Farmersville, IL

Silly Rhymes

4+

LEARNING OBJECTIVES

The children will:
1. Identify and produce rhyming words by sounding out patterns.
2. Learn the names of different animals.

Materials

pictures of things that rhyme with different animals featured in "Down by the Bay"

CD with the song "Down by the Bay"

VOCABULARY

animal names	same	song
rhyme	sing	sound

WHAT TO DO

1. Play "Down by the Bay" for the children. When the song mentions an animal, such as "moose," have the children try to guess what may rhyme with it.

2. As an extension, provide pictures of things that rhyme with the animals. If the children are unable to come up with a rhyming word, show the pictures to the children and they can then choose a word that rhymes.

TEACHER-TO-TEACHER TIP

- Rather than focusing on spelling patterns, concentrate on sound patterns. The sillier the better. For example, Moose and "roose," even though "roose" is not a word.

SONGS

"Cluck, Cluck, Red Hen"
"Old MacDonald Had a Farm"

ASSESSMENT

Consider the following:
- Can the children identify images that rhyme with the names of the animals mentioned in "Down by the Bay"?
- Do the children learn the song?

Children's Books

If You Give a Mouse a Cookie by Laura Joffe Numeroff

Old MacDonald Had a Farm by Colin and Jacqui Hawkins

Whose Sound Is This?—Chirps, Clicks, and Hoots by Nancy K. Allen

Eileen Lucas, Fort McMurray, Alberta, Canada

The Little Green Chameleon

LEARNING OBJECTIVES

The children will:
1. Learn the words to a song about chameleons.
2. Make up movements to the song.

Materials

VOCABULARY

brown   chameleon   green   red   snake

WHAT TO DO

1. Teach the children the following song.

    The Little Green Chameleon by Laura Wynkoop
    (Tune: "The Itsy Bitsy Spider")
    The little green chameleon
    Climbed high up in a tree.
    Out came a snake
    To see what he could see.
    The little green chameleon
    Turned brown and red and then
    The big snake slid away,
    And he turned to green again.

2. Explain to the children that chameleons can change colors, if they are confused by the words of the song.
3. After the children become comfortable with the words to the song, challenge them to make up hand or body movements that go along with each line.

Children's Books

Chameleon, Chameleon by Joy Cowley
Chameleons Are Cool: Read and Wonder by Martin Jenkins
Rain Forest Babies by Kathy Darling

ASSESSMENT

Consider the following:
- Do the children know the words to the song?
- Do the children understand that chameleons can change color to match their surroundings?

Laura Wynkoop, San Dimas, CA

Little Farmer's Animal Action Vowels

5+

LEARNING OBJECTIVES

The children will:
1. Learn vowel sounds.
2. Learn about animals.
3. Improve their motor skills.
4. Learn action verbs.

Materials

hazard cones or
 masking tape
poster board
colored markers
cards
cups

VOCABULARY

animal names   verb   vowel

PREPARATION

- On a poster, write the words of the song below with each action verb in green, each animal in blue, and each vowel in red.
- Label cups "name" and "action."
- Mark off a movement area with cones or tape. (Tell each child that she is in a bubble and if she gets too close to another child her bubble will burst.)

WHAT TO DO

1. If appropriate, do this activity with one or two children at a time.
2. The green words on the poster are action verbs because you can do them around the room. Individual children can demonstrate the actions.
3. Discuss each animal. Say the animal word and the vowel sound in the word.
4. Teach the children the "Old MacDonald's Animal Action Vowels" song.

Little Farmer's Animal Action Vowels by Kathy Stemke
(Tune: "Old MacDonald Had a Farm")

A little farmer had a vowel, A-E-I-O-U.
And on his farm the antelope dance,
* A-E-I-O-U*

With an a, a, here, and an a, a, there,
Here an a, there an a, everywhere an a, a,
The little farmer had a vowel, A-E-I-O-U.

5. Make cards with one animal name or action word. Challenge the children to place the cards in the correct name cup or action cup.

ASSESSMENT

Consider the following:
- Can the children identify the animals by name?
- Can the children differentiate between a name and an action?

Kathy Stemke, Mount Airy, GA

Children's Books

If You Give a Mouse a Cookie by Laura Joffe Numeroff
Old MacDonald Had a Farm by Colin Hawkins and Jacqui Hawkins
Whose Sound Is This?—Chirps, Clicks, and Hoots by Nancy K. Allen

Index of Children's Books

Index

ALSO AVAILABLE

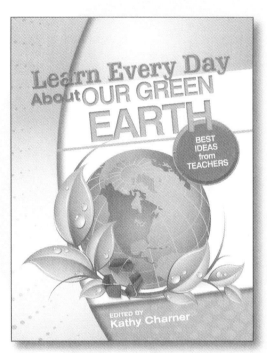

ISBN 978-0-87659-127-7
Gryphon House / 12015 / PB

ISBN 978-0-87659-128-4
Gryphon House / 11500 / PB

ALSO AVAILABLE

ISBN 978-0-87659-088-1
Gryphon House / 13467 / PB

ISBN 978-0-87659-090-4
Gryphon House / 15573 / PB

ISBN 978-0-87659-092-8
Gryphon House / 16247 / PB

ALSO AVAILABLE

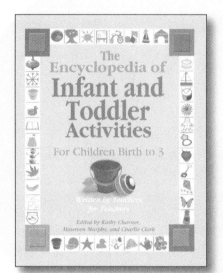

ISBN 978-0-87659-013-3
Gryphon House / 13614 / PB

ISBN 978-0-87659-237-3
Gryphon House / 13963 / PB

ISBN 978-0-87659-238-0
Gryphon House / 14964 / PB

+3ISBN 978-0-87659-285-4
Gryphon House / 18595 / PB

ALSO AVAILABLE

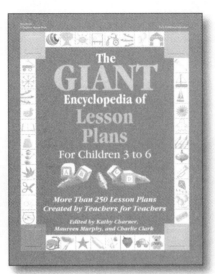

ISBN 978-0-87659-068-3
Gryphon House / 18345 / PB

ISBN 978-0-87659-166-6
Gryphon House / 19216 / PB

ISBN 978-0-87659-012-6
Gryphon House / 15002 / PB

ISBN 978-0-87659-003-4
Gryphon House / 12635 / PB

ALSO AVAILABLE

ISBN 978-0-87659-001-0
Gryphon House / 11325 / PB

ISBN 978-0-87659-193-2
Gryphon House / 18325 / PB

ISBN 978-0-87659-181-9
Gryphon House / 16413 / PB

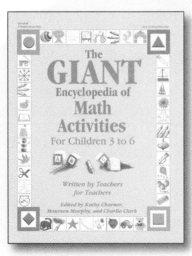

ISBN 978-0-87659-044-7
Gryphon House / 16948 / PB

ISBN 978-0-87659-209-0
Gryphon House / 16854 / PB